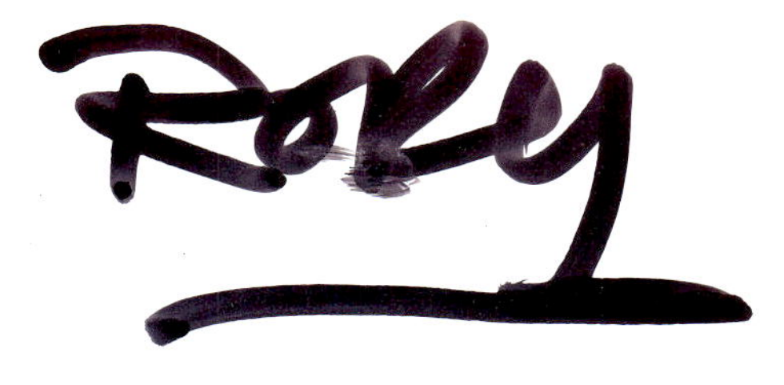

Contents

2 Director's Foreword
3 Sponsor's Foreword
4 The Prizes
5 The Judges

Schweppes Prize
6 First Jens Lucking
8 Second James Reeve
10 Third Angus Fraser
12 Fourth Henrik Knudsen

Deloitte Award
14 Winner Paul Plews

16 Exhibitors

Director's Foreword

The 2004 *Schweppes* Photographic Portrait Prize demonstrates the vitality and excellence of portrait photography. This year's call for entries exceeded all expectations. With nearly 8,000 images submitted by more than 2,500 photographers from around the world, the submission represents a huge international enthusiasm for photographic portraiture in every possible guise and with the widest possible interpretation.

The *Schweppes* Prize is all about people. People who may appear intriguing, defiant, relaxed, or just ordinary, but all of them willing to be portrayed. It is also about the outstanding skills of the photographers: their intelligence and diligence. Selecting just sixty-one prints from nearly 8,000 gave the jury a considerable but exhilarating challenge to find the very best images. Many of the portraits submitted will have lasting value for both the subject and the photographer. They record much more than just a moment in time – they capture something of the spirit of those photographed, in a format that can be shared with friends, family or viewers. Yet for the small number that we could choose for display, there had to be something additional, something exceptional in the quality of the print and the nature of the image – whether in the pose, surroundings or lighting – that was communicated to the jury and which might also be intriguing and enjoyable for those visiting the exhibition.

I should like to thank all of the many photographers who submitted to this year's Prize. I offer many congratulations to Jens Lucking, James Reeve, Angus Fraser and Henrik Knudsen who won the *Schweppes* prizes and to Paul Plews, the worthy winner of the Deloitte Prize. This is awarded for a portrait photograph by a photographer aged twenty-five or under and represents the continuing successful partnership between Deloitte and the Gallery. I am very grateful to Deloitte for their support for our contemporary photographic displays and acquisitions.

I want to give special thanks for the support of Coca-Cola *Schweppes* as the overall sponsors of the Prize and the exhibition. Their support for contemporary photographers is exemplary and they have created a wonderful new showcase for those working in the field of portraiture.

I should also like to thank my fellow judges: Magda Keaney, Sarah Kent, Terry O'Neill, Terence Pepper and Lola Young. They were unstinting in their attention and care, while being robust in debate. My thanks also go to Stephen Allen, Pim Baxter, Naomi Conway, Claire Everitt, Susie Foster, Clare Freestone, Roger Hargreaves, John Haywood, Beatrice Hosegood, Ruth Müller-Wirth, Kathleen Soriano, Hazel Sutherland, Rosie Wilson and other National Portrait Gallery staff, as well as the designers NB: Studio, and the interviewer Richard McClure, for all their hard work on the exhibition and the catalogue.

Sandy Nairne, Director,
National Portrait Gallery

Sponsor's Foreword

Photography is a medium like no other. It has the ability to invigorate, astound and move you. When images are presented in a new context, we are often forced to reconsider the over-familiar in a new and surprising light.

Schweppes has long been a strong supporter of creativity and the arts, working with artists such as Alison Jackson to create the *Sch ... You Know Who?* advertising campaign, which captured look-alikes of well known personalities in imaginary off-guard moments.

We are proud to sponsor the 2004 *Schweppes* Photographic Portrait Prize, allowing fresh contemporary talent the chance to truly sparkle. This year's exhibition promises to be both refreshingly inspirational and pleasurably thought-provoking, giving viewers a tantalising glimpse into the vast diversity of human spirit and character.

We hope you enjoy the exhibition.

Julia Goldin, Marketing Director, Coca-Cola Great Britain

The Prizes

Schweppes Photographic Portrait Prize

The *Schweppes* Photographic Portrait Prize is open to photographers from around the world aged eighteen or over.

The first prize winner is Jens Lucking, who receives £15,000

The second prize winner is James Reeve, who receives £1,000

The third prize winner is Angus Fraser, who receives £1,000

The fourth prize winner is Henrik Knudsen, who receives £1,000

Deloitte Award

The Deloitte Award is for the best portrait taken by a photographer aged twenty-five or under. The Award forms one part of a larger contemporary photography-based partnership between Deloitte and the National Portrait Gallery, which started in autumn 2003. Deloitte are supporting several areas within the Gallery's ground floor contemporary photographic displays, as well as donating an acquisition fund for photographic portraits of figures from public life, and helping the Gallery to develop its UK touring programme of contemporary photography from the Collection.

The winner is Paul Plews, who receives £5,000

If you would like to join the mailing list to receive an entry form for next year's *Schweppes* Photographic Portrait Prize, please send your full contact details to:

Schweppes Photographic Portrait Prize 2005
Marketing Department
National Portrait Gallery
St Martin's Place
London WC2H OHE

The Judges

Chair: Sandy Nairne, Director, National Portrait Gallery
'Given the scale of this year's submission, the judges had to be especially rigorous as so many good portraits shone out. But in the final choice I think we found a range of images, whether of individuals or groups, from the United Kingdom and around the world, that represents the continuing vitality and excellence of portrait photography.'

Sarah Kent, Writer and Critic
'It is a tribute to the success of the *Schweppes* Photographic Portrait Prize that this year 7,915 images were submitted by 2,615 photographers – more than double than that for 2003. But trying to select around sixty exhibits from such a wealth of material was a nightmare, especially as the quality of the work was so high. When it came to choosing a winner and runners up, there was no hope of easy agreement, so all decisions were made by voting – which is as it should be. Two things are certain: that the exhibition will be exceptionally good and that people are bound to disagree with our choices. That's what makes competitions so infuriating yet so worthwhile – they generate debate. As for the judging process, it was an exhausting but hugely rewarding challenge. Thank you to all those photographers who entrusted their work to us and gave us such a difficult but stimulating task.'

Magda Keaney, Formerly Curator of Photographs, National Portrait Gallery, Canberra
'Being a judge was a unique opportunity to scrutinize as large a cross section of contemporary portraiture at one time as I'm ever likely to. Not looking for one particular element, I approached the experience as openly as possible. The portraits I was most taken with appealed to me instantly and intuitively. This might have been on an aesthetic, technical or an intellectual level. Portrait photography assumes a powerful place in contemporary culture and can be a pivotal site for the presentation and exploration of ideas, the documentation of personal history or the idealisation and commemoration of public events and figures. With this in mind, I wanted to be inspired, challenged and excited by what I saw without it fitting into any prescribed form or framework.'

Terry O'Neill, Photographer
'The *Schweppes* Portrait Prize is the best photographic show I have ever seen and judging it was the most difficult job I have had to do in the past four years.'

Lola Young, Freelance Consultant in the Cultural Sector, Former Head of Culture, Greater London Authority
'Many people might find the idea of looking at thousands of photographic images and making the case for their choice a daunting prospect, but I really enjoyed it. I try to approach the work with an open mind, and listen to the reasons why the other judges feel the way they do about a particular image, or photographic genre. I really like to try to get a sense of what it was that the photographer wanted to say about her/his subject. There are no hard-and-fast rules about what works and what doesn't for me – sometimes less is more, sometimes it's not quite enough. But when we got to the shortlist and all the judges agreed on a particular photograph, it was a magic moment.'

Terence Pepper, Curator of Photography, National Portrait Gallery
'Viewing nearly 8,000 photographs and deciding amicably which sixty-one should be in the final selection seemed at the outset an impossible task to complete in just two days. However, a consensus was happily achieved and the photographs illustrated in this catalogue point to a contemporary pictorial Zeitgeist that relates to photographic portraiture.'

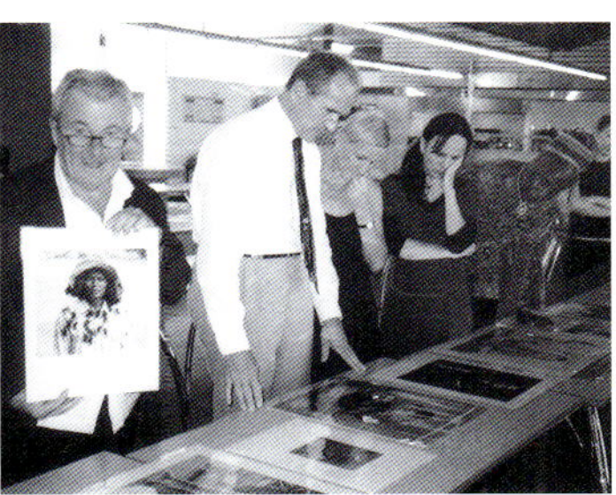

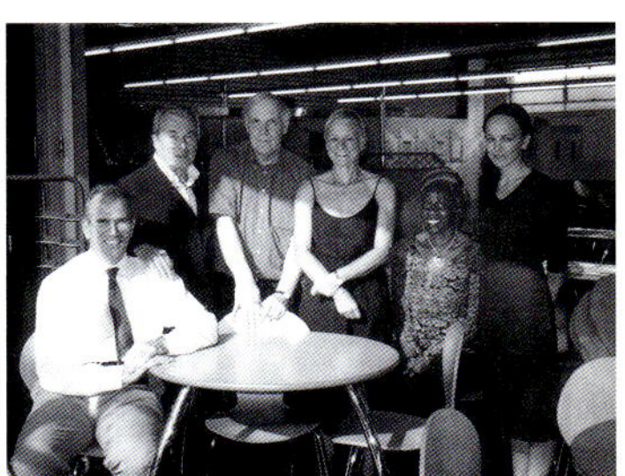

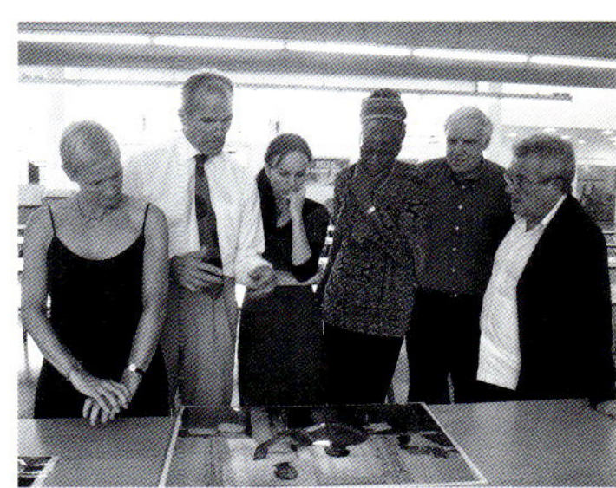

Schweppes First Prize Winner Jens Lucking

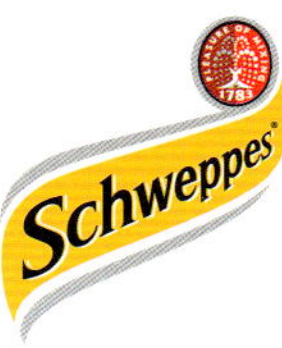

Born into a family of engineers in Minden, Germany, Jens Lucking began taking photographs aged ten, after receiving his first camera from an uncle. His early efforts focused exclusively on his other childhood passion – cars. 'As a kid, I must have taken thousands of pictures of cars,' he recalls. 'Perhaps that's why I love Jacques-Henri Lartigue. I had the same youthful obsession with photography and automobiles.'

As a teenager, Lucking was torn between car design and photography as a career, eventually opting for the latter – much to his parents' disapproval. Their displeasure increased when, after training in Germany, he moved to London in 1996. 'I took all my savings, said my goodbyes and headed for the UK,' explains Lucking, now aged thirty-two. 'Six months later, all the money was gone and my parents were nagging at me to come home and get a proper job.'

Deciding to stick it out, Lucking was thrown a lifeline when he 'hassled' car photographer Chris Bailey into hiring him as his assistant for two years – a job that brought him financial stability and the opportunity to indulge his twin passions once more. While continuing to shoot advertising campaigns for various car manufacturers, Lucking now devotes more time to non-commercial work. In 2001 his portraits of nude women in public places were shown at London's Cable Street Gallery. That same year he exhibited a portrait of a Jamaican neighbour in the John Kobal Photographic Portrait Award.

Since 2002 Lucking has been employed by Getty Images, working on assignments around the world for the photo agency. His winning entry in this year's *Schweppes* Photographic Portrait Prize, *Tokyo*, was taken during his first visit to Japan. Shot with a Hasselblad 503CW, using ringflash to prevent shadow, the portrait shows three schoolgirls – Erina, Reina and Zyuria – whom Lucking met through a mutual friend.

'The photograph is set up but I didn't want it to appear too posed or fashion-like,' he explains. 'Part of my style is to push naturalism a bit, but I still like things to look believable and realistic. I'd never met these women before, but I hope I've managed to capture something of their characters. They all came across as strong females so that's how I show them – self-confident, almost arrogant. I was determined to avoid that cute, demure, Japanese schoolgirl thing, and I think this portrait is the antithesis of that.'

Interviewed by
Richard McClure

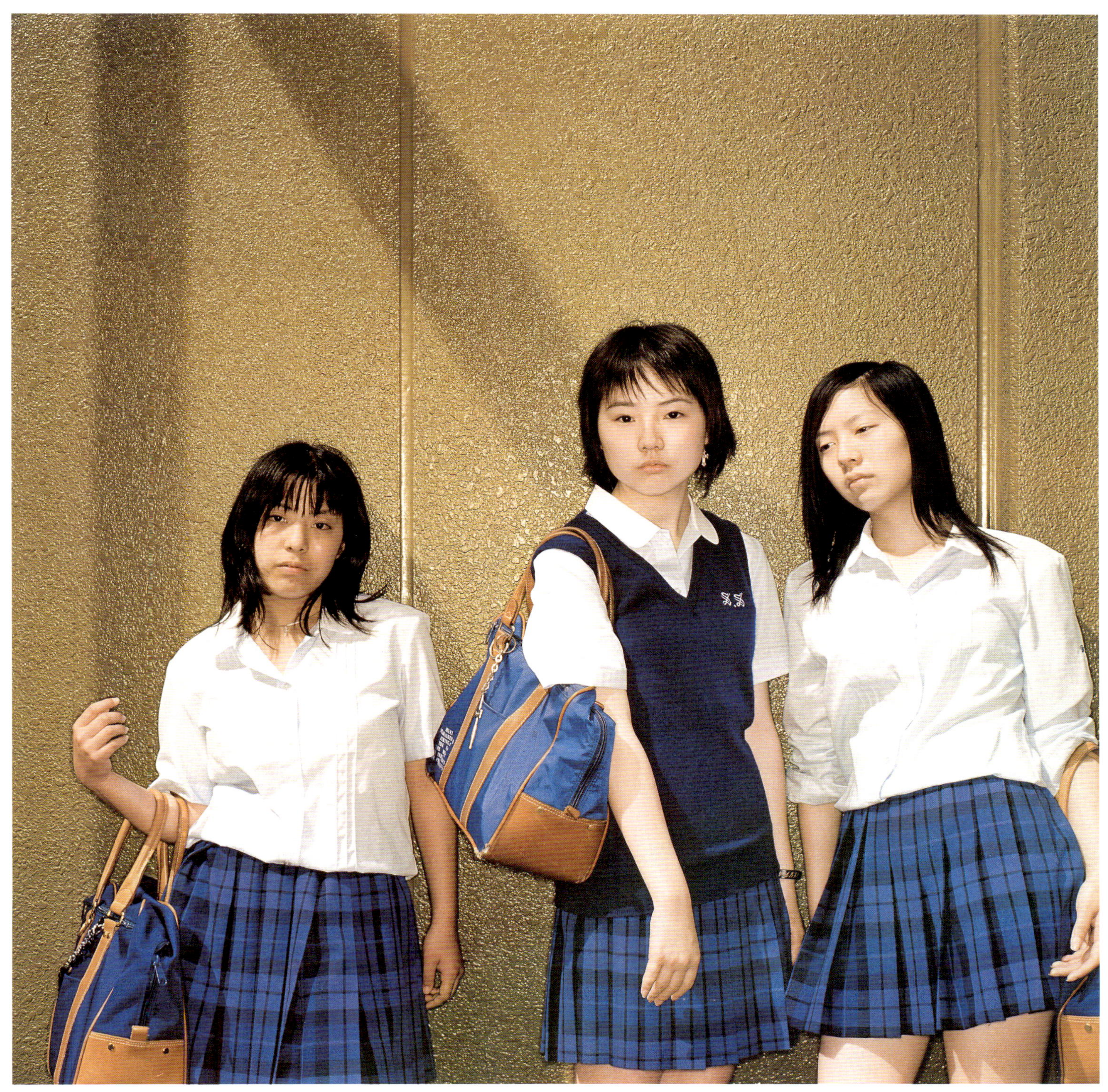

Schweppes Second Prize Winner James Reeve

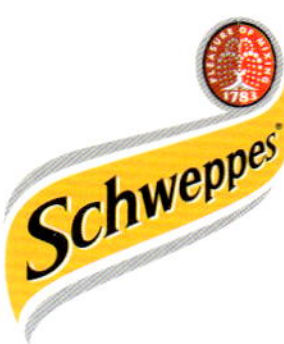

When London-born photojournalist James Reeve travelled to Afghanistan in May 2004 his aim was to document everyday activities that had previously been banned by the Taliban. Having taken photographs of a girls' school and people flying kites, Reeve then turned his lens onto a team of Kabul footballers, many of whom had lost limbs from land-mines.

Pictured on playing fields next to the city's notorious Ghazi stadium, once a venue for executions, the amputee team had just finished a match against an able-bodied side, narrowly losing 2-1. 'Sport, including football, was heavily curtailed by the Taliban,' explains 30-year-old Reeve. 'Men playing the game were forbidden from wearing shorts, and spectators were not allowed to cheer for their team. They could only shout Allah Akhbar (God is Great). It was quite amazing to watch them play. In the photograph, their faces show an obvious satisfaction that they could still compete against an able-bodied team. A storm was brewing as I took the picture, which brought a beautiful, painterly quality to the light. Soon after, the heavens opened and poured down onto the pitch.'

Working in the humanitarian style of photographers such as James Nachtwey and Sebastião Salgado, two of his inspirations, Reeve spent time befriending the players, gradually establishing the rapport that he believes is a vital ingredient of his work. 'As a photojournalist you sometimes feel you are running in and out of people's lives – by the nature of the job you have to be quick,' he says. 'You need an ability to communicate with people and gain their trust. And you have a duty not to betray that trust. I wanted to come away from Afghanistan showing something positive.'

A freelance photojournalist since 1999, Reeve has travelled to more than thirty-five countries and contributed to a variety of magazines, including features about Canada and Vietnam published in *Condé Nast Traveller* and a recent photo essay on Chernobyl for *Esquire*. Shot with a Mamiya Rangefinder, the Afghanistan project was only the second occasion that Reeve had used medium format for his reportage work, having previously preferred 35mm.

Last year, Reeve and seven other photojournalists established the photographic collective Forum. Their first group show took place at London's Proud Gallery in August 2004 and they are now planning a major project together. 'There's a real range of styles in the group, but what we share is a similar ethos. There's no financial side to it, we're a bunch of friends who hang out, discuss ideas and provide mutual support. At times, photography can be a lonely profession.'

Interviewed by Richard McClure

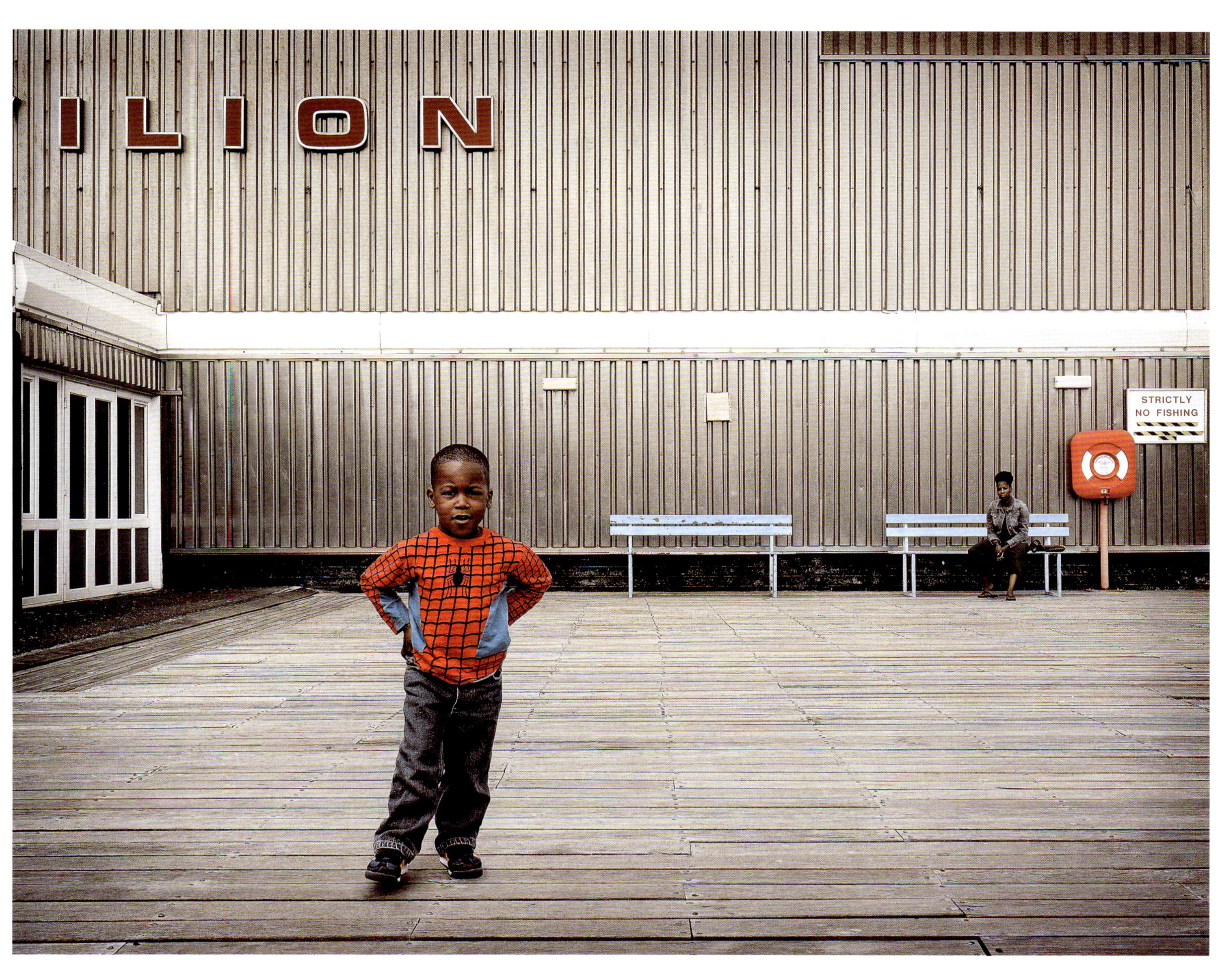
ILION
STRICTLY
NO FISHING

Schweppes Fourth Prize Winner Henrik Knudsen

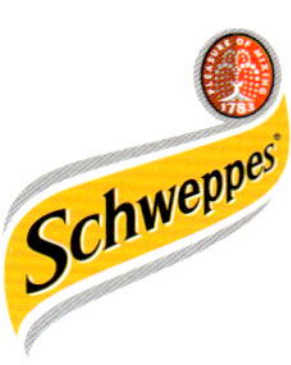

Digital technology may have speeded up the photographic process for most professionals, but Henrik Knudsen was in no great hurry to take his *Schweppes* entry, *Jonathan I*. After persuading the owner of a Clerkenwell noodle bar to let him shoot on the premises, the Danish-born photographer then spent a number of weeks meticulously searching for the right person to fill the space, eventually choosing model Jonathan Stout.

'I find people in various ways,' explains 37-year-old Knudsen. 'Sometimes they come from agencies, sometimes they're friends or people I've stopped in the street. I saw quite a few people before I chose Jonathan. Because he's a busy model and musician I had to wait several months before I could arrange the shoot. I could have photographed other people in that specific location, but I only wanted him. The way he looked was exactly right.'

Using a medium-format Hasselblad, Knudsen arranged and lit the portrait to enhance the natural light from the window. The image was then manipulated using Photoshop to control the colours and contrast. Having studied computer science before switching to photography in his mid-twenties, his technological expertise has proved a useful tool. 'I recently closed down my old black-and-white dark-room because I hadn't used it for about five years,' he says. 'Computers are the modern-day dark-room, though I don't like my pictures to look manipulated.'

Moving to London in 1992, Knudsen assisted other photographers before finding freelance work shooting book covers for the publishers Macmillan and Hodder Headline. Now established as an advertising photographer, his recent clients include Apple and Sony Playstation. In April, his campaign for Nokia won a silver Association of Photographers Award.

Currently, he is devoting time to non-commercial pictures – a series on the American West Coast and another on his home country, Denmark. 'For me, capturing the essence of a place is very important. Even in my portraits, I hardly ever shoot people on a plain background. My portraiture is as much about the location as it is about the model. Lately, I've been more influenced by cinema than photography and most of my pictures have a narrative content. I like them to tell small stories about people or places. The picture of Jonathan is a little like that – I like the way small visual clues in his tattoos work with the images on the wall. More than anything, my aim is to make the uninteresting interesting or find beauty in the mundane. I want to reveal things that people perhaps haven't noticed before.'

Interviewed by
Richard McClure

Henrik Knudsen

Jonathan I
May 2004

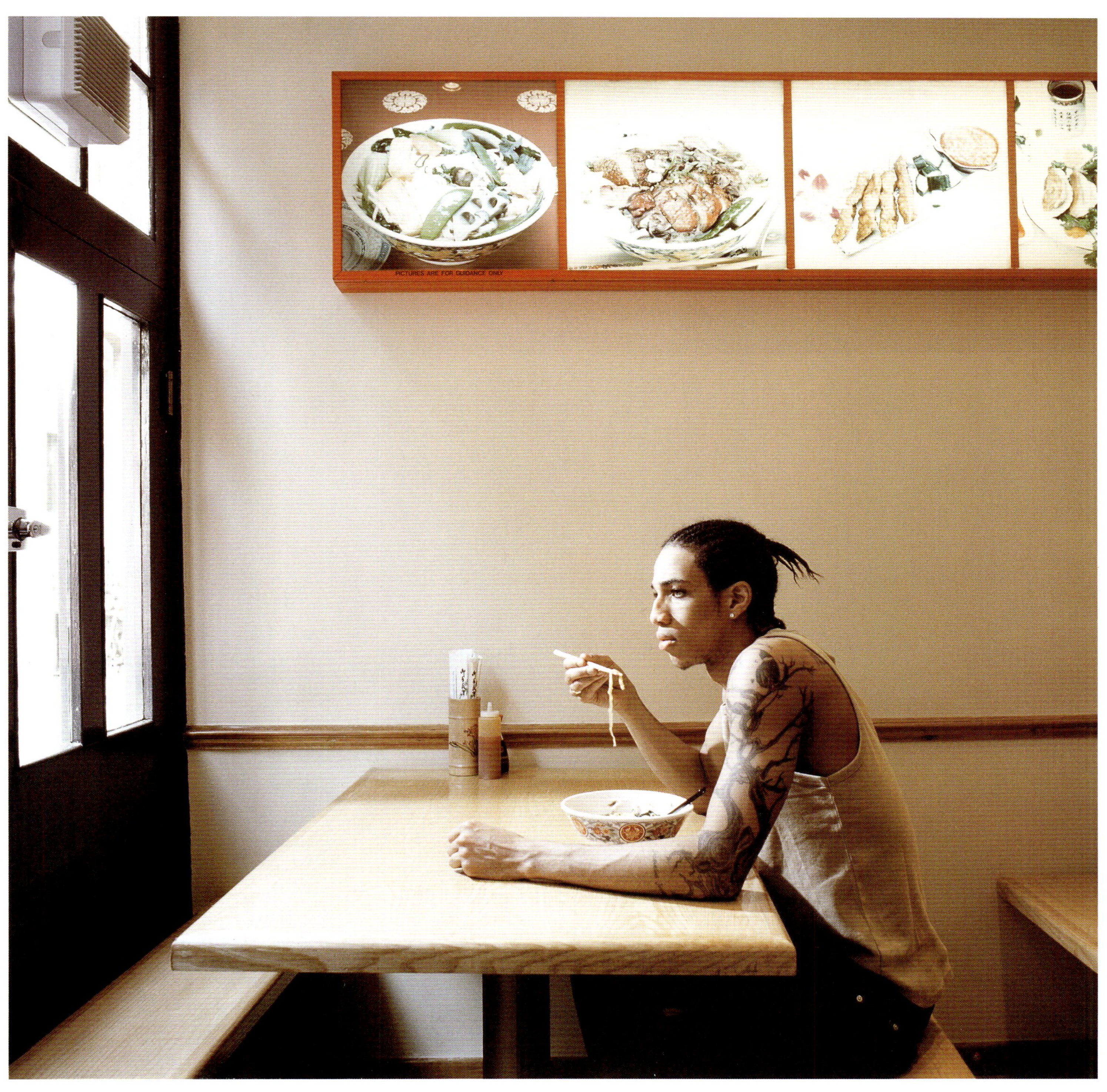

Deloitte Award Winner Paul Plews

Winner of the Deloitte Award for the best portrait taken by a photographer aged twenty-five or under, Paul Plews graduated last year with a BA (Hons) in Photography from Blackpool and the Fylde College. The winning portrait, *Untitled*, is taken from his degree show portfolio, a series of random encounters with strangers on the Blackpool seafront.

Approaching anyone who 'looked like they had a story to tell', Plews persuaded local people to pose in front of a white backdrop he'd rigged up in a nearby backstreet, photographing his subjects with a RB 6 x 7. 'I prefer taking portraits outside the studio because people are less defensive,' explains 24-year-old Plews. 'You get a more natural, uninhibited response, which means you're able to get closer to their real selves. Blackpool is full of fascinating characters. It's a place where people get washed up.'

While most of his sitters took an interest in the project and were happy to divulge personal details, the subject of his winning entry preferred to keep her anonymity. 'She refused to tell me her name and I know virtually nothing about her, which I quite like in a way. It brings a degree of ambiguity to the picture. Rather than telling people everything about her, it's nice to let them make up their own minds.'

Brought up in Ashington, Northumberland, Plews spent his childhood 'hanging about on waste ground and building sites' and began taking photographs for an art A-level project – a series of images about derelict shipyards on the Tyne. 'I'm proud of my working-class upbringing and I've incorporated the industrial surroundings of my childhood into my work,' he says. 'Perhaps subconsciously my pictures – including the Blackpool portraits – explore what it feels like to be northern.'

Since graduation Plews has moved to London, where he's now 'on a very steep learning curve' as assistant to photographer Bob Carlos Clarke. Despite his relocation, however, he continues to focus on themes of industrial decline, regularly returning to Northumberland to photograph the last working deep mine in the north-east.

'The biggest influence on my work is Chris Killip's 1980s photographs of people scavenging for sea coal and I suppose there's a similar melancholy feel to my pictures,' he says. 'I've landed on my feet working for Bob Carlos Clarke, doing photo shoots of celebrities such as Nell McAndrew and advertisements for Guinness, but my own work is very different. I'm not interested in the glamour; I'm interested in the people who have to clean up afterwards.'

Interviewed by
Richard McClure

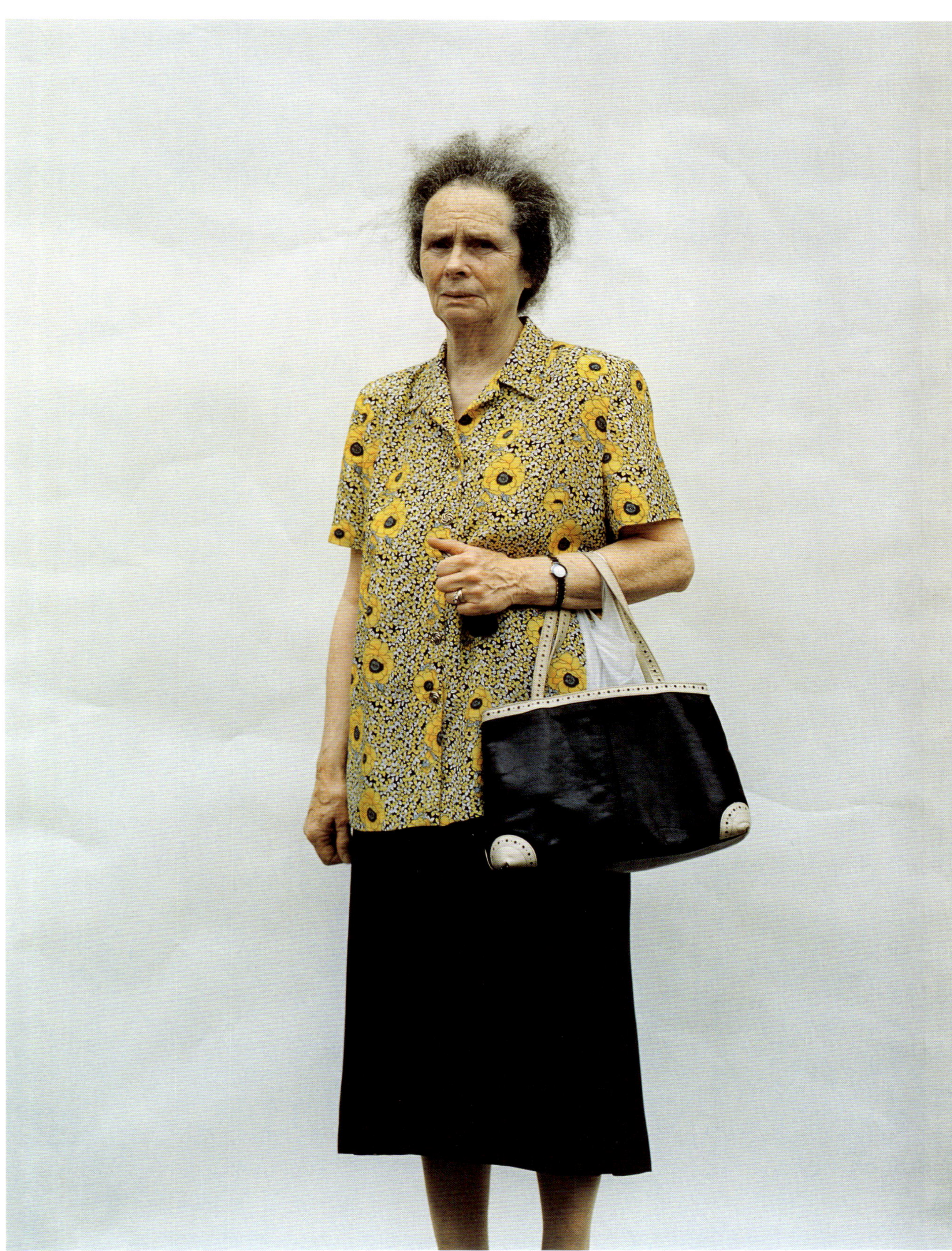

Exhibitors

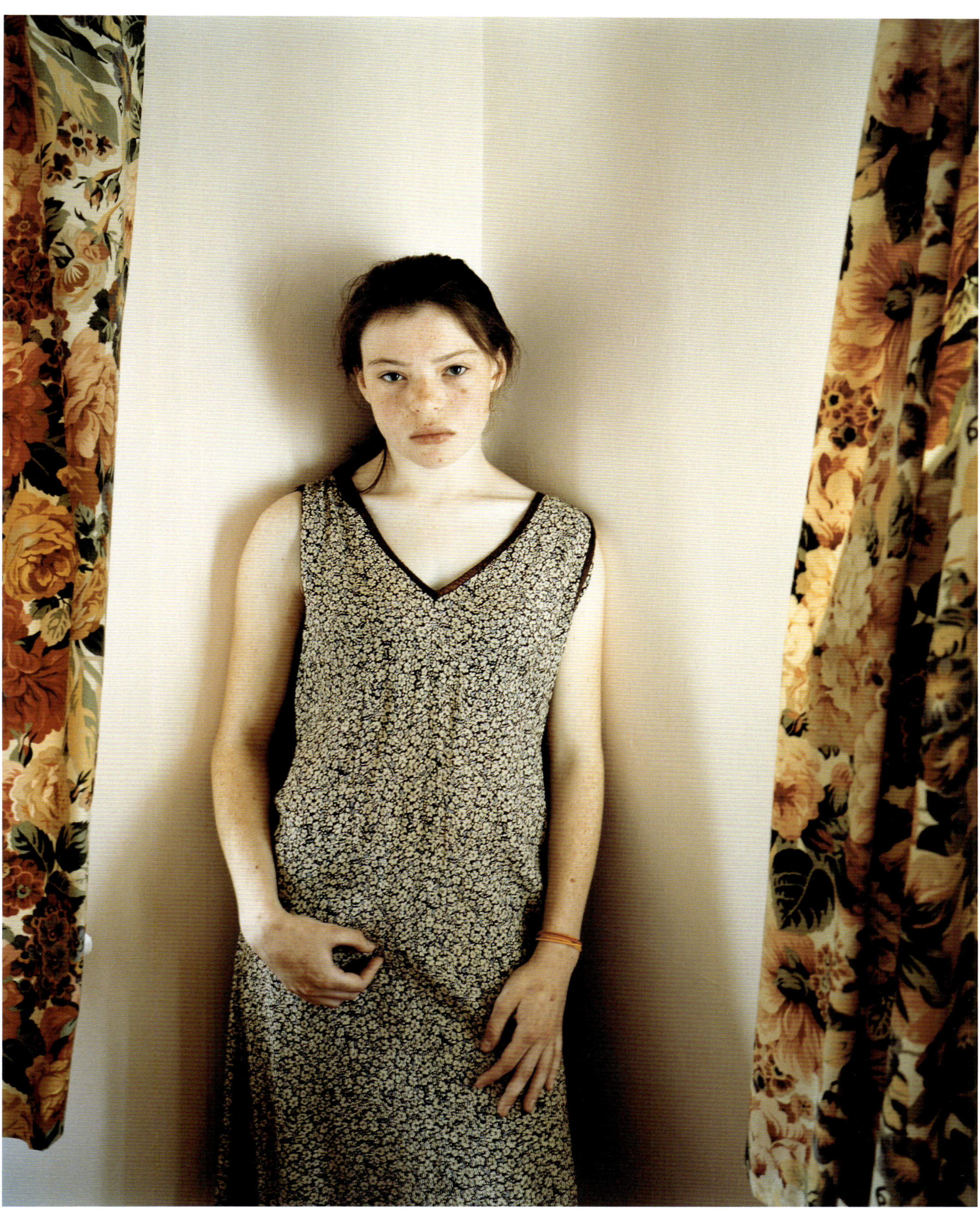

Kyna Gourley

Anne Marie O'Neil
Age 13
(Mother: Adhesive Arachnoiditis)
from the series
Growing Care
July 2003

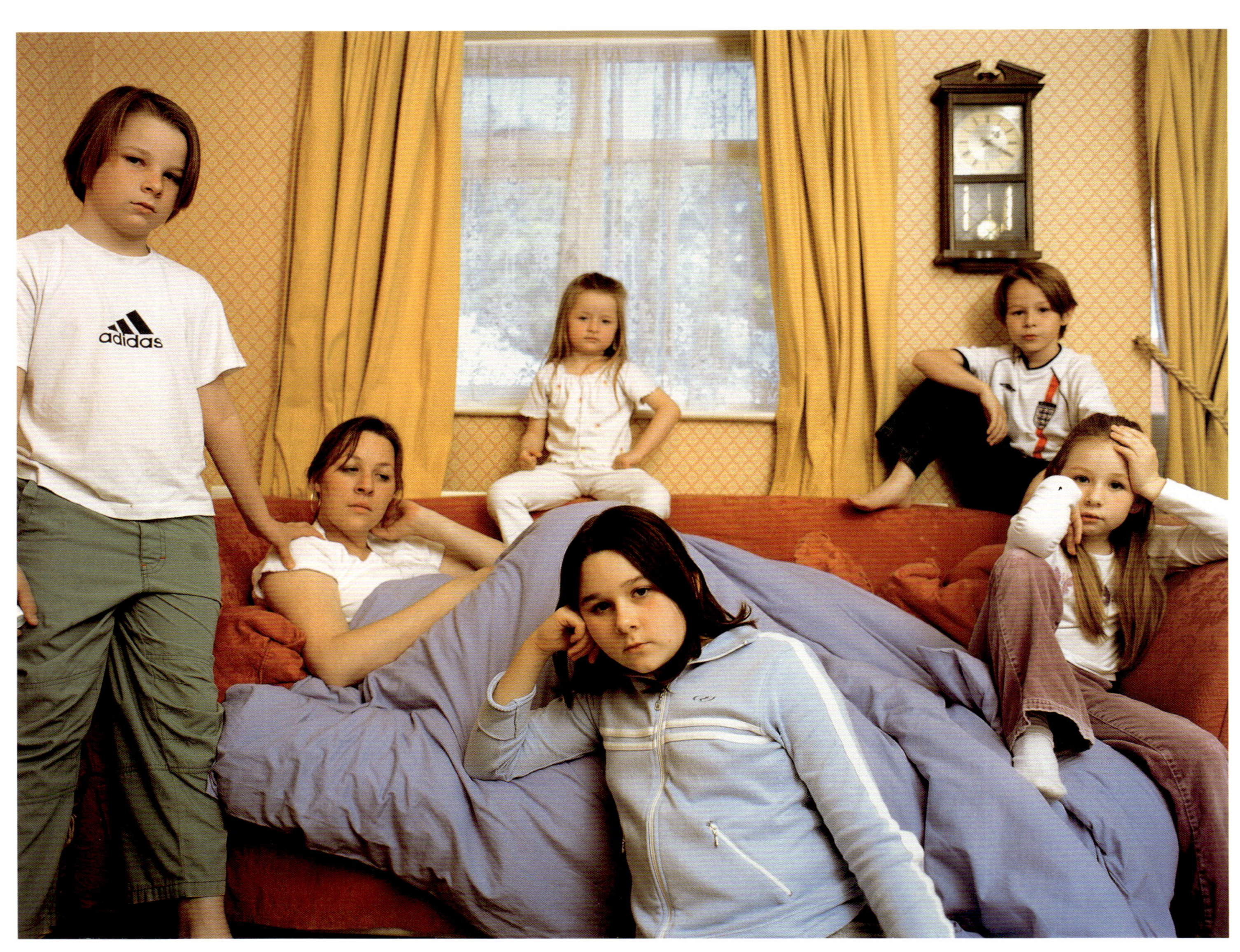

Lucy Levene

Untitled (Dinner)
November 2003

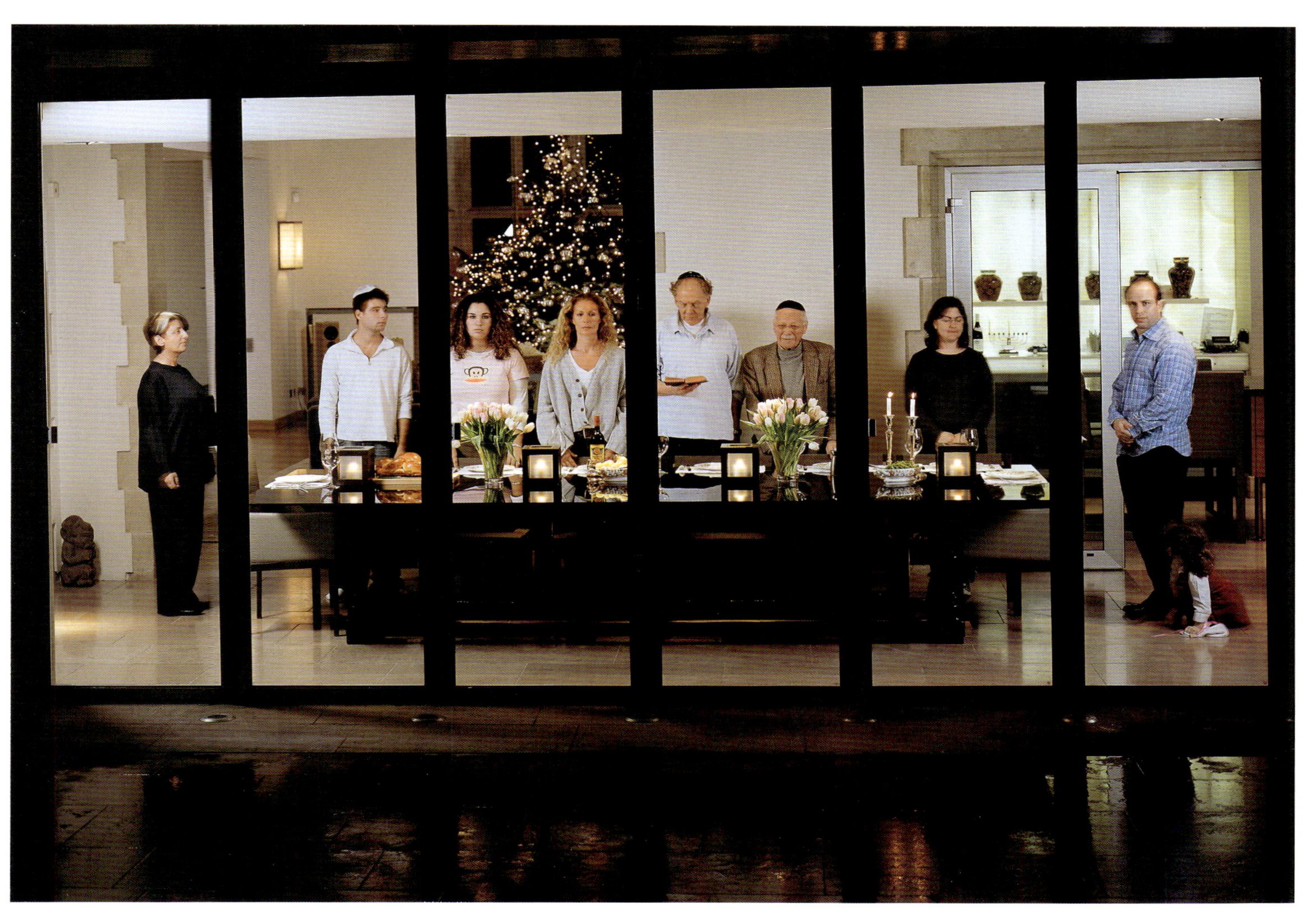

Sacha Maric

Hannah *from the series* Teenager, Kelly Osbourne Concert at the Electric Ballroom, Camden
June 2003

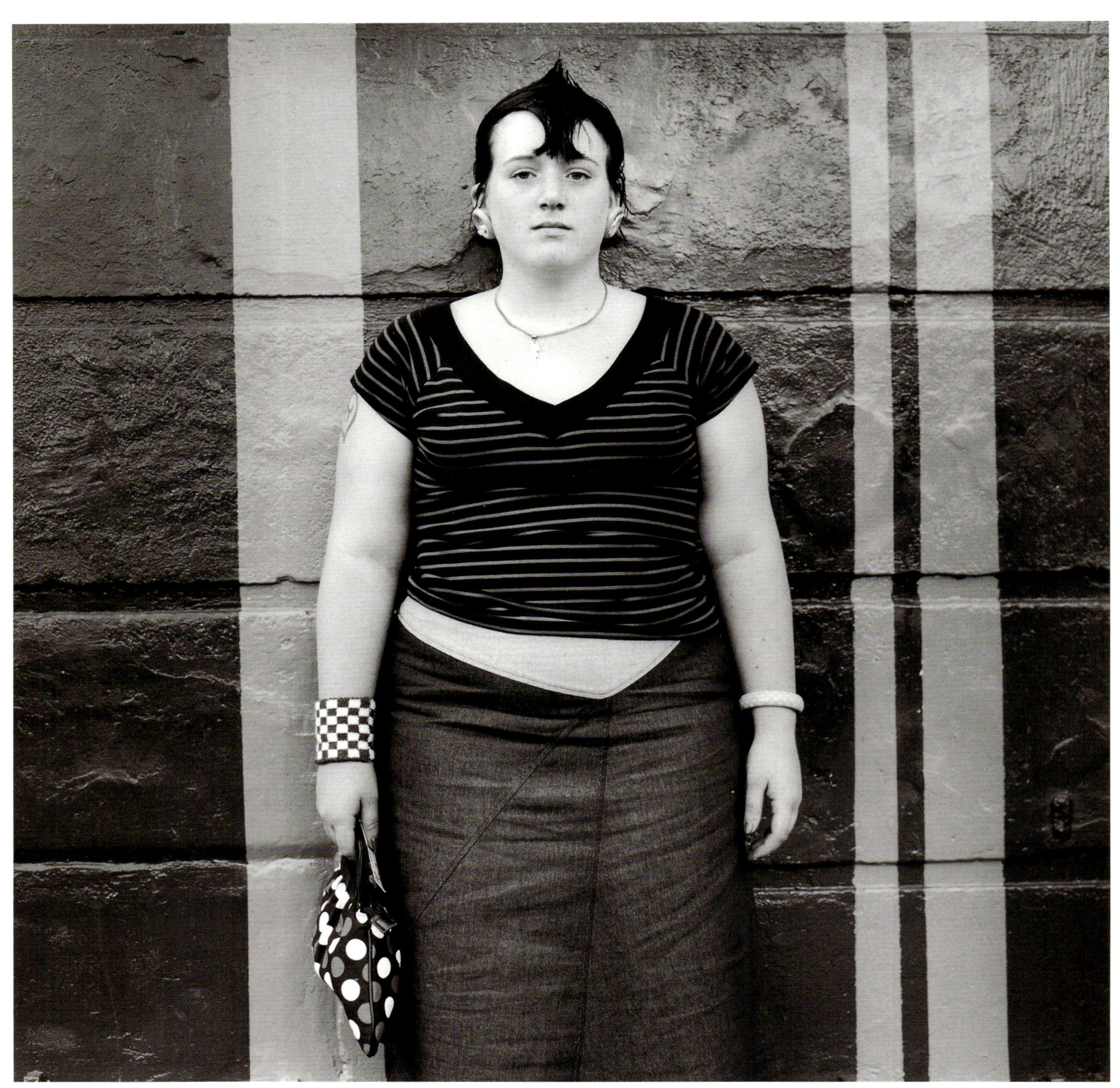

Sacha Maric

Hare Coursing Spectators
from the series
The Annual Waterloo Cup, Hare Coursing Tournament, Great Altcar
June 2003

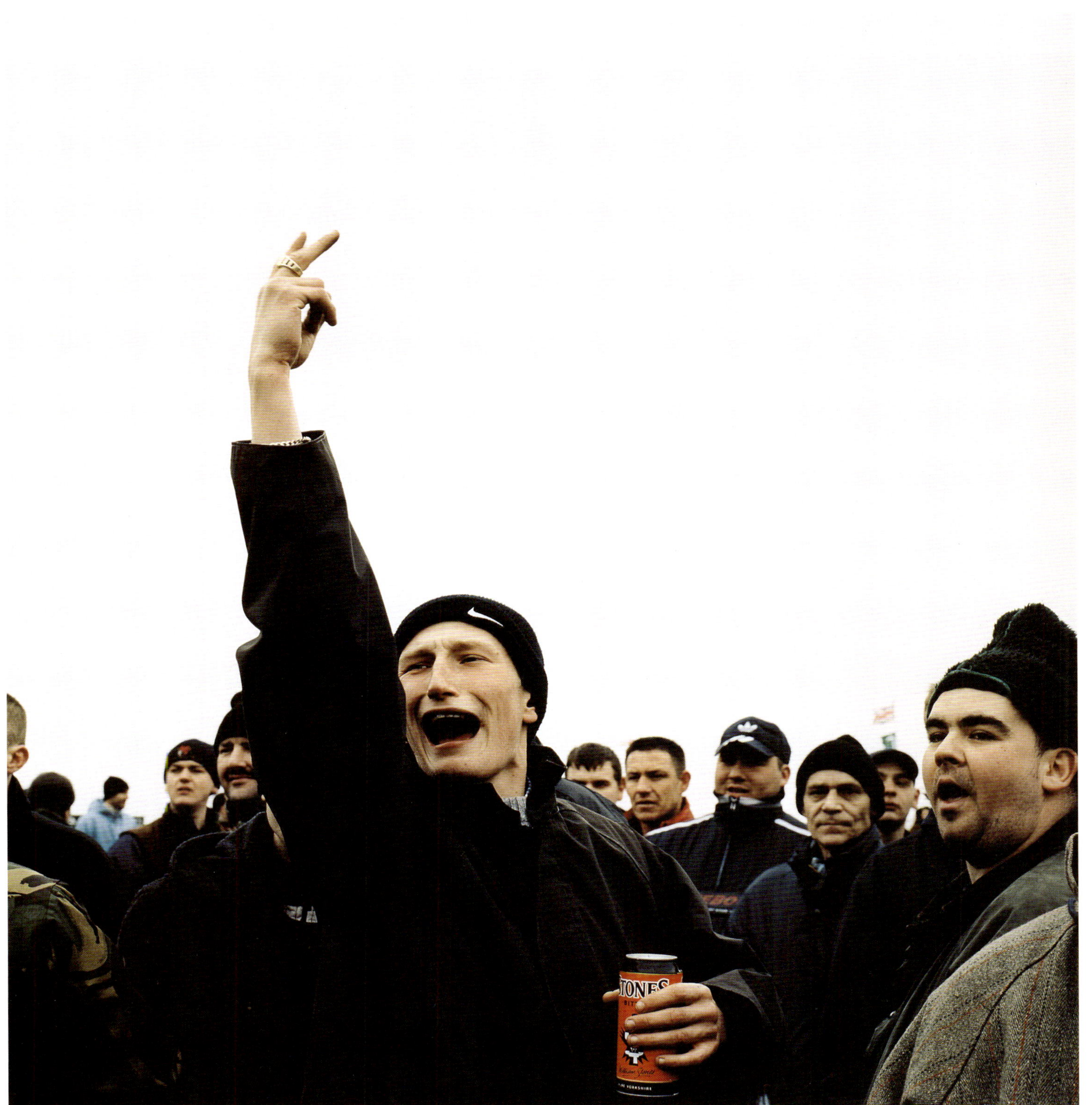

Emma Critchley

Portrait I *from the series*

Portraits May 2004

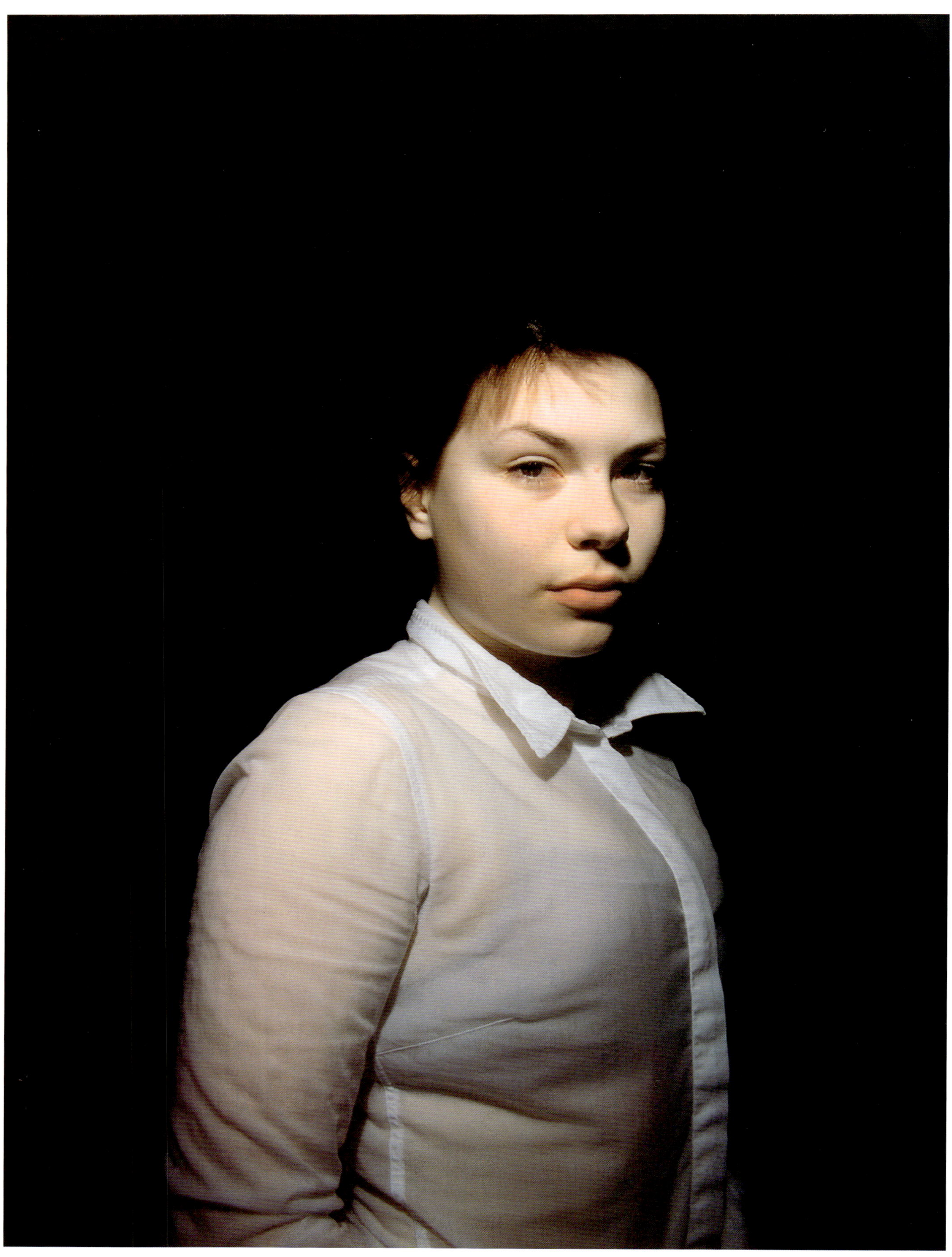

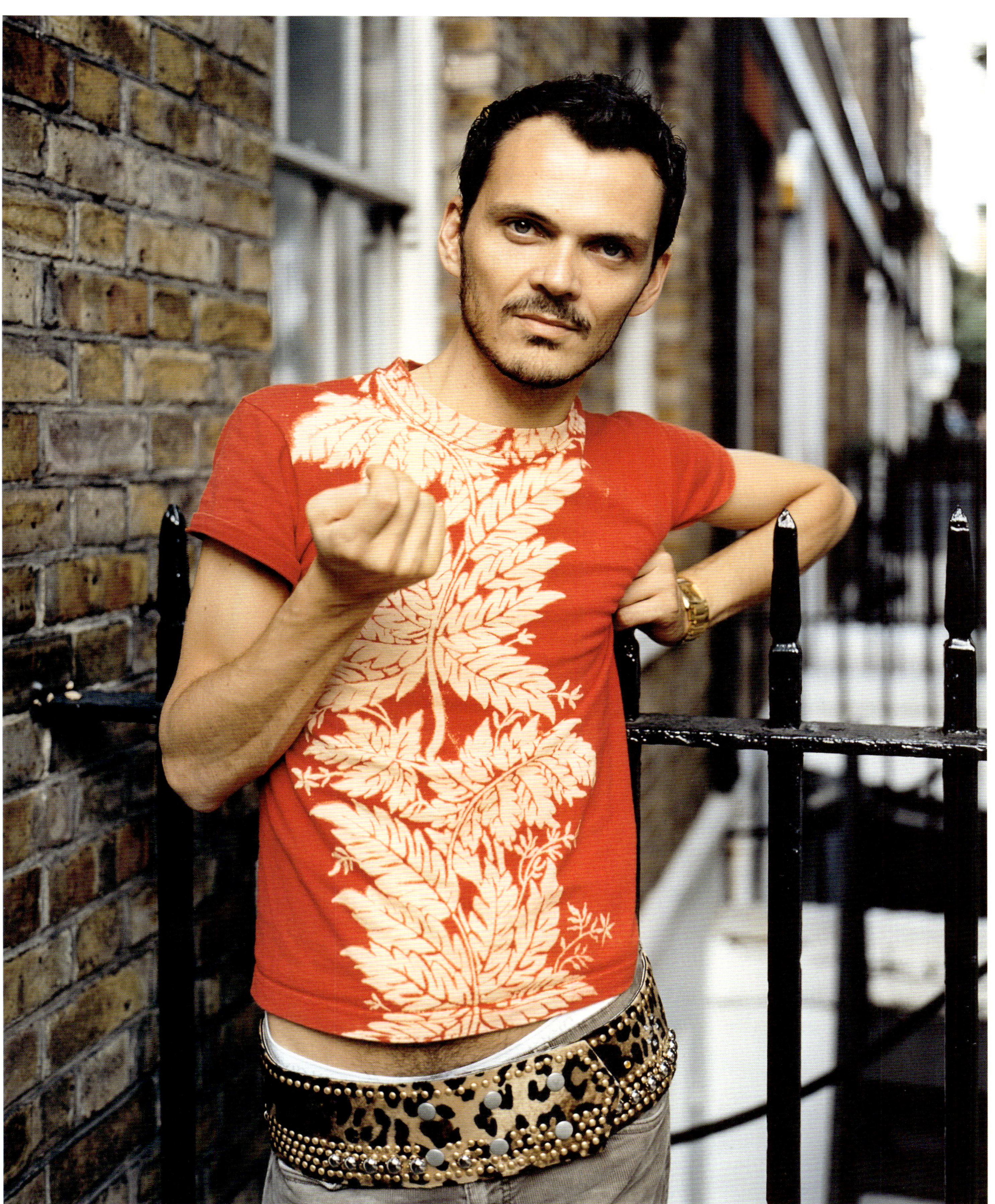

Dirk Lindner Hadley
July 2004

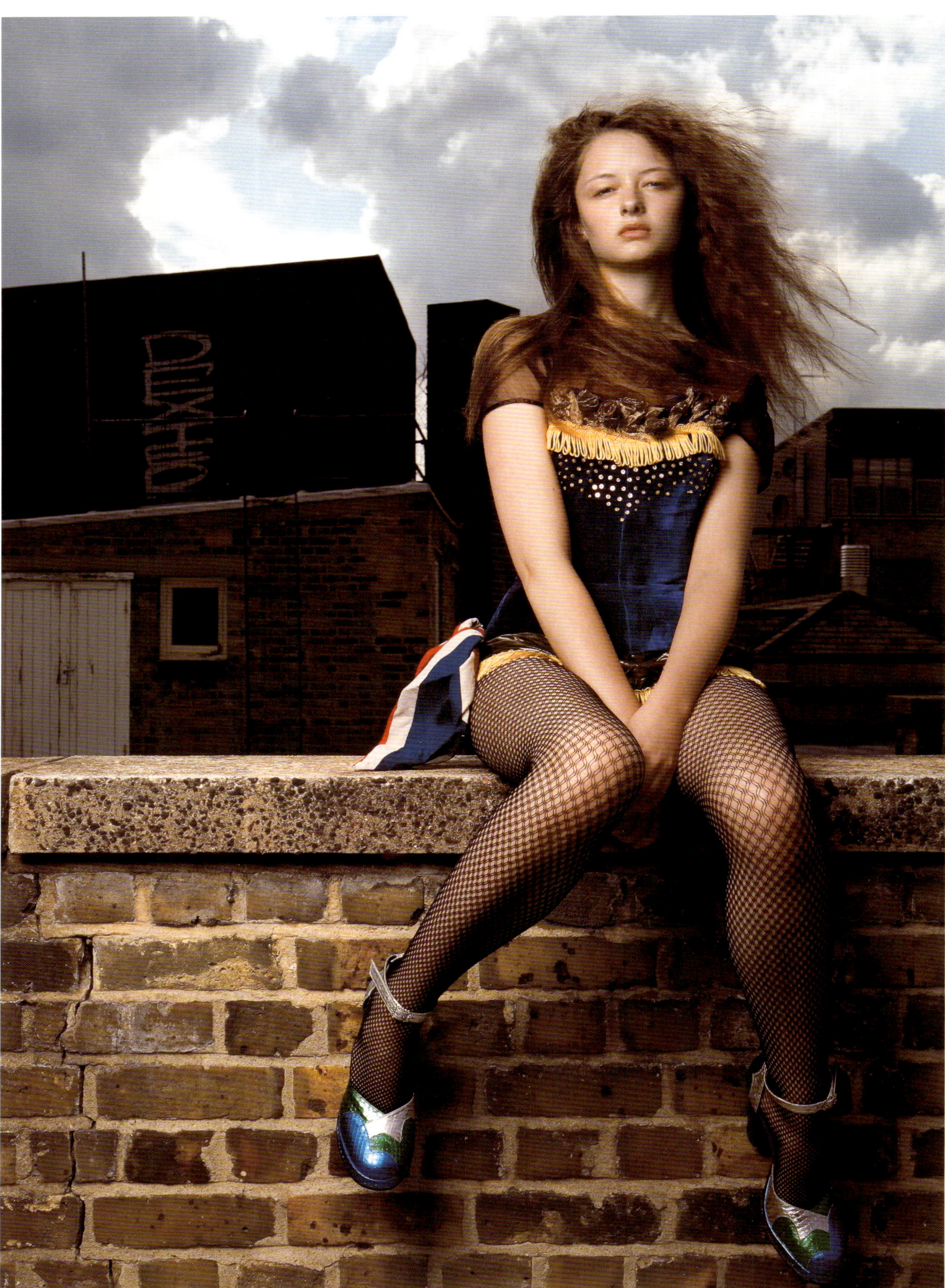

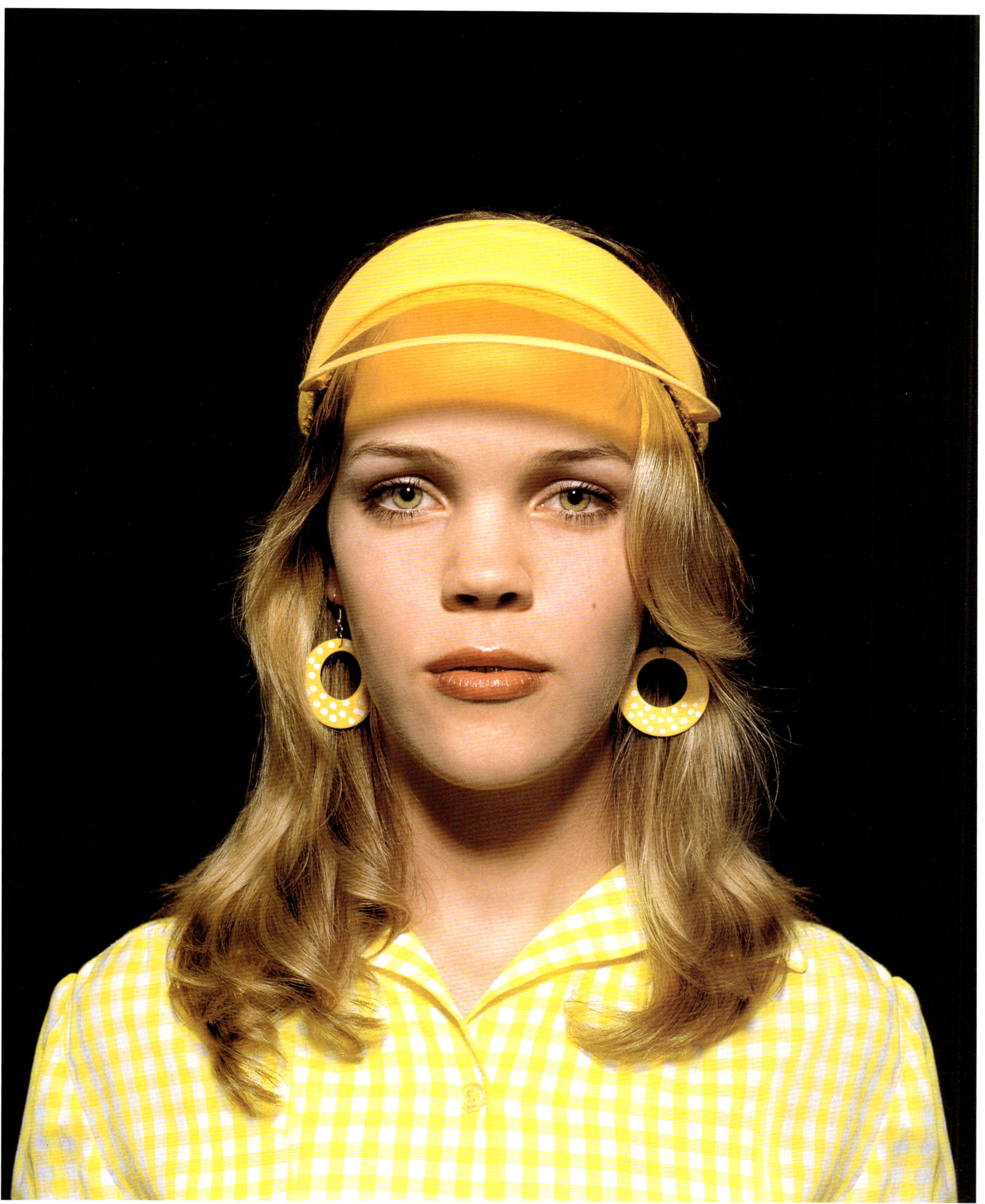

Zoe Roussadana

Olga S, Waitress *from the series* One Man (Show)
August 2003

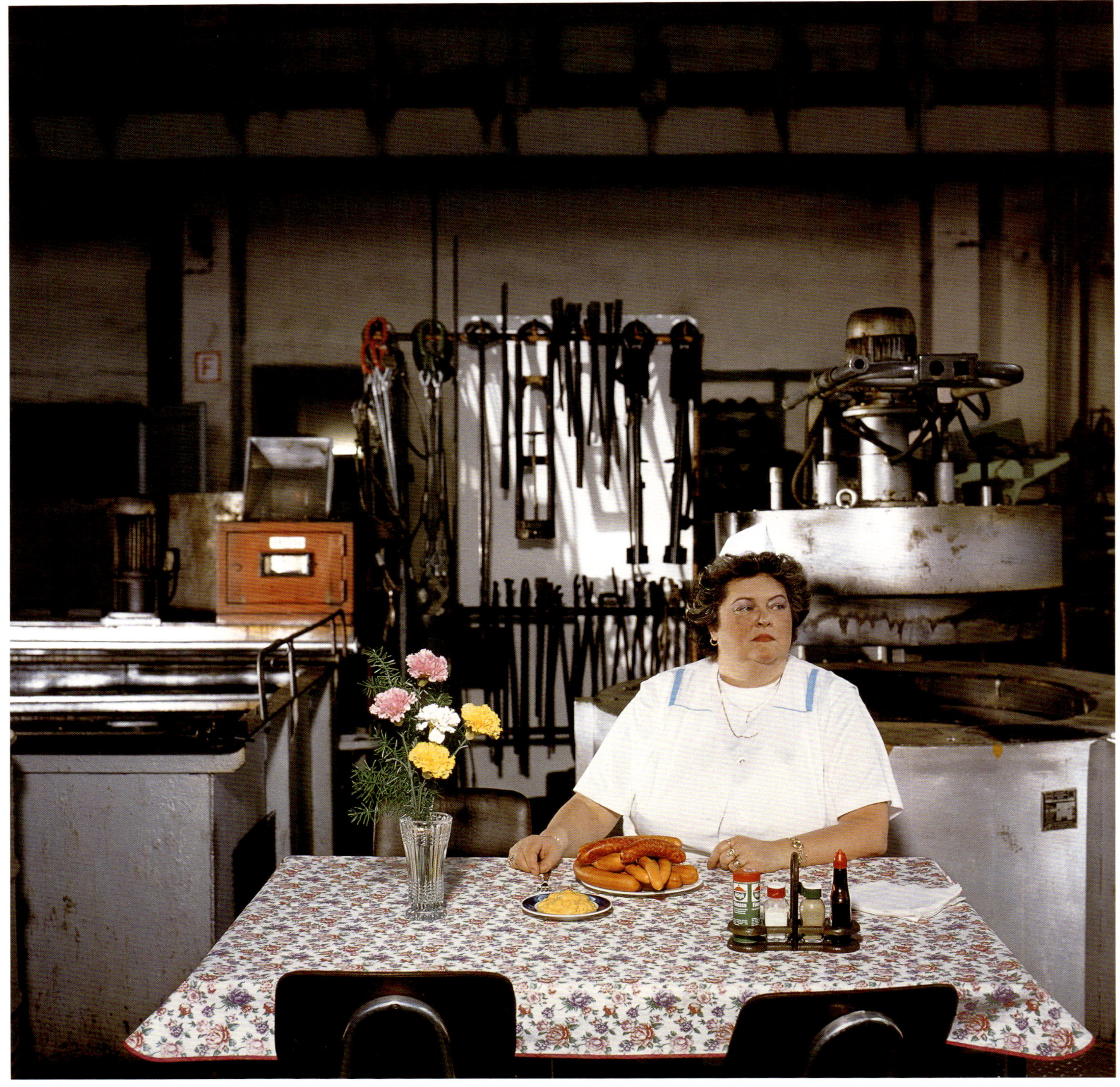

Anthony Luvera

Gary McLoughlin *from the series* Assisted Self-portraits July 2004

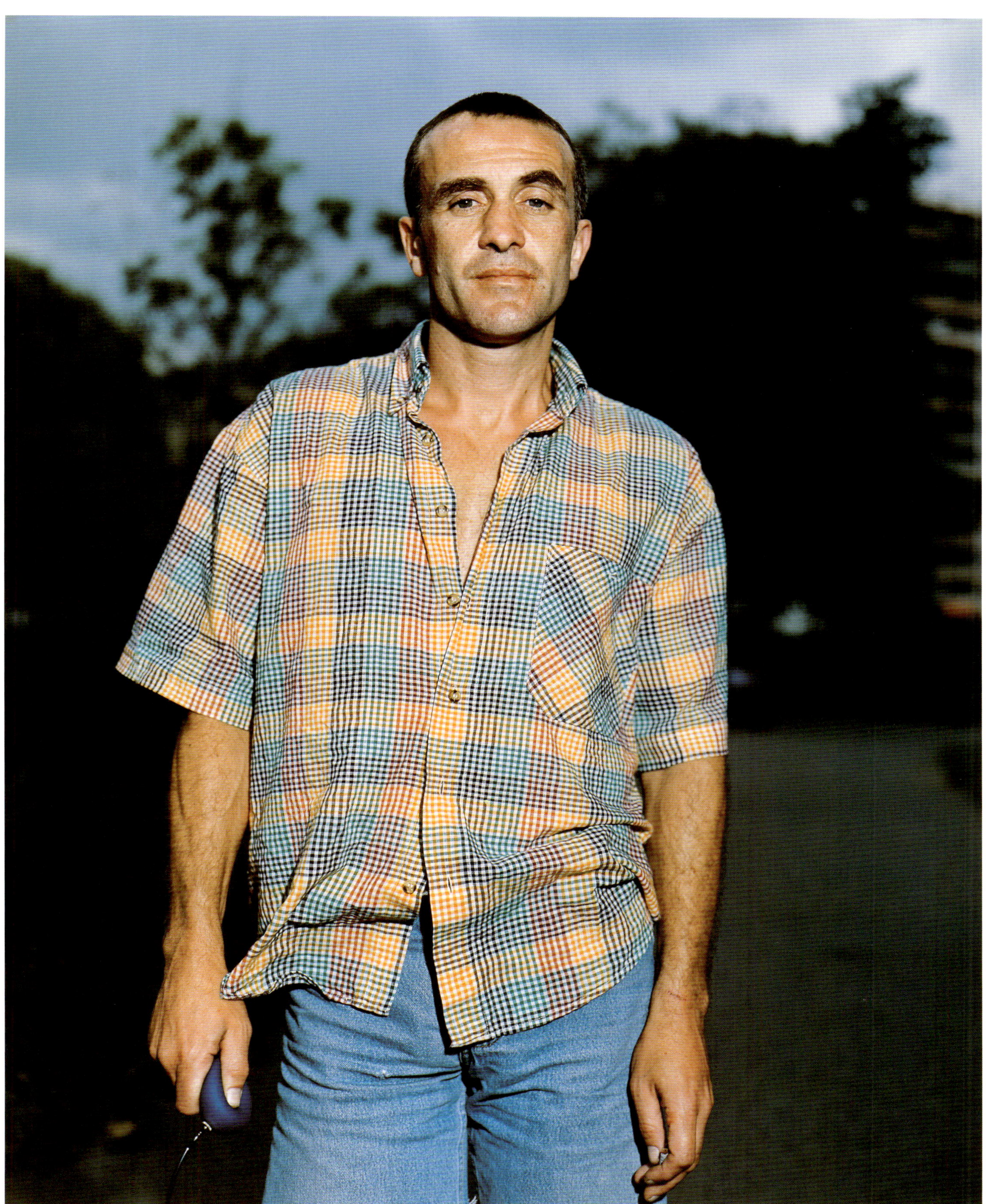

Igor Emmerich Paul *from the series* Androgynous July 2004

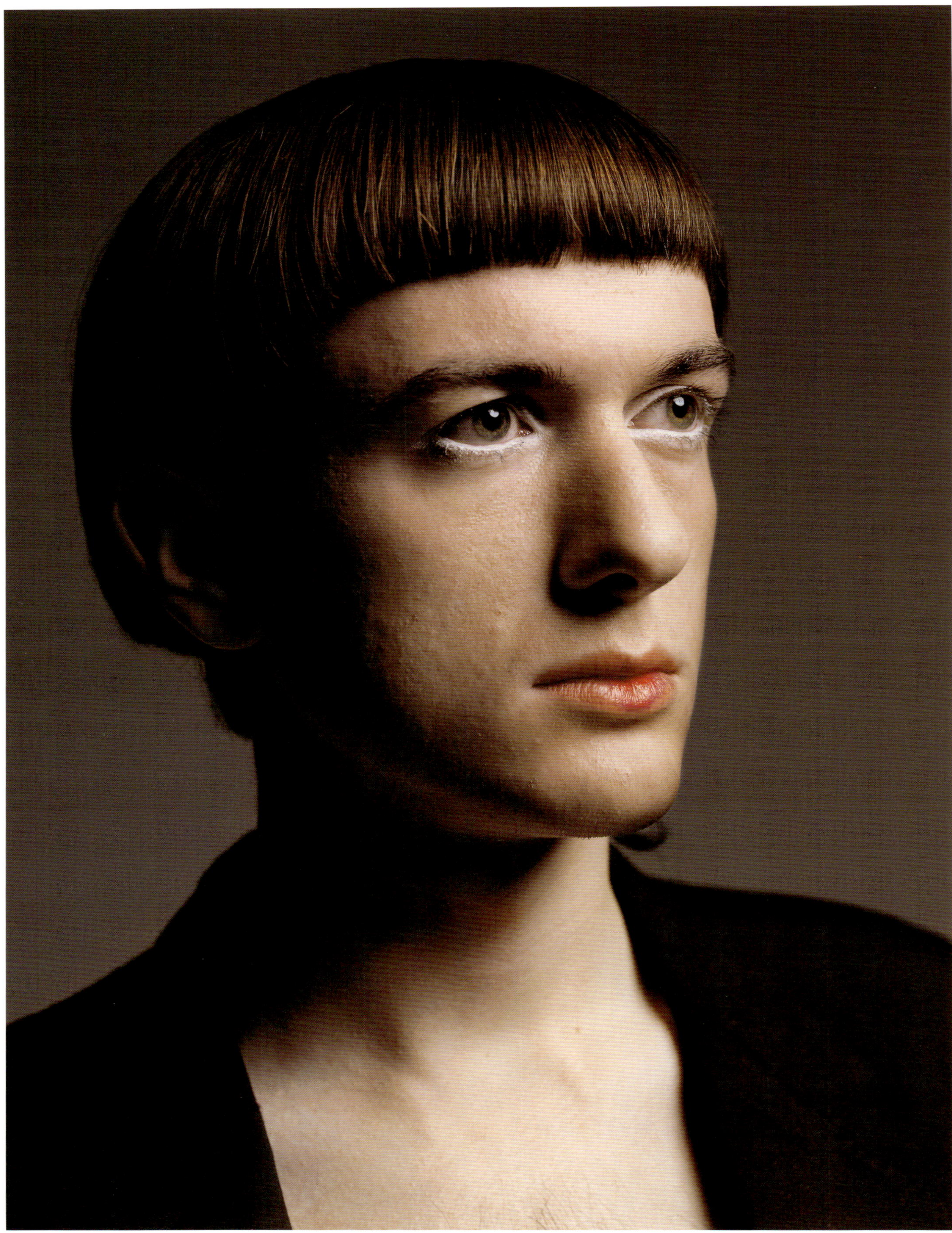

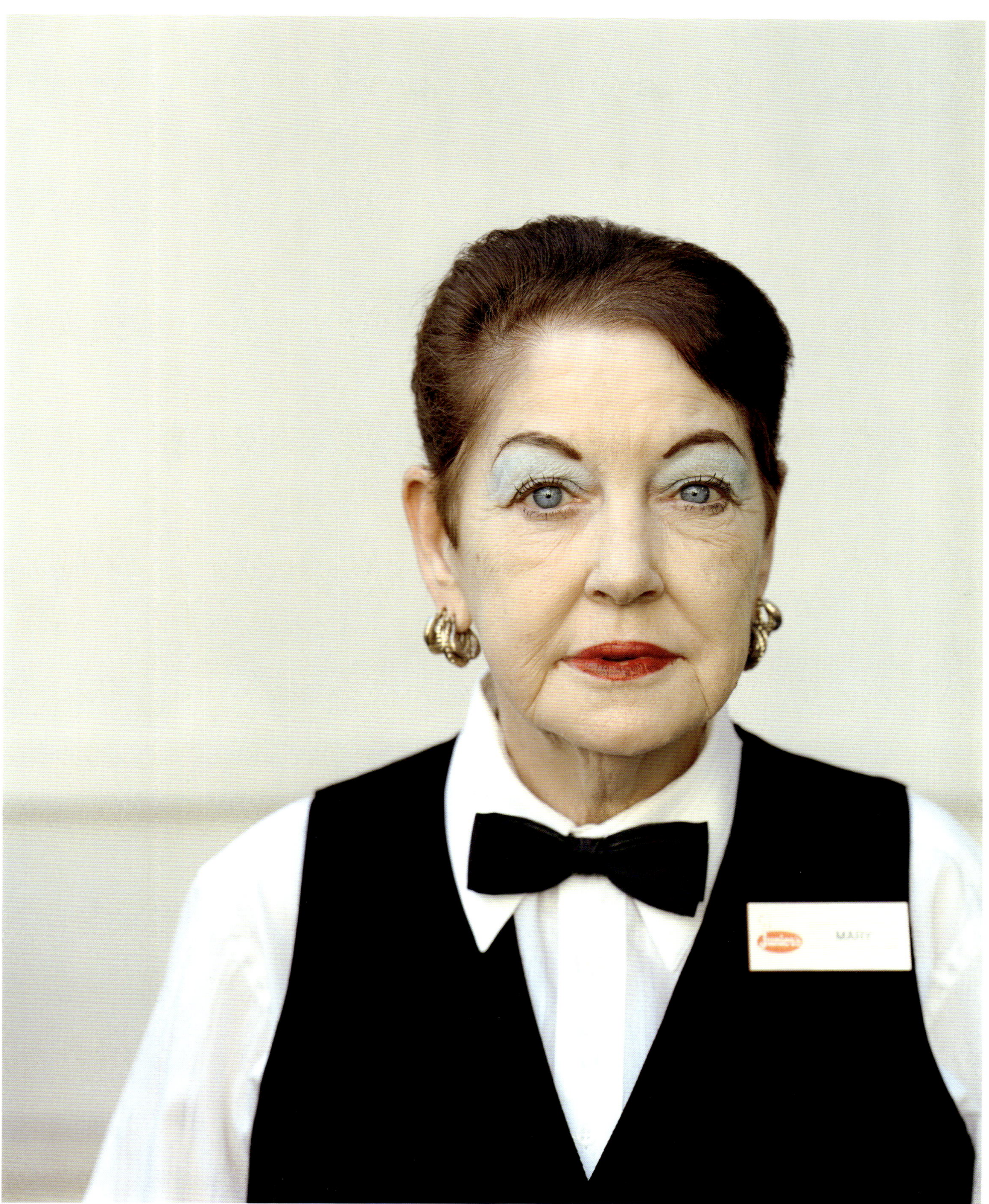

Karina
Sutherland
Whitelaw

The Knockout
March 2003

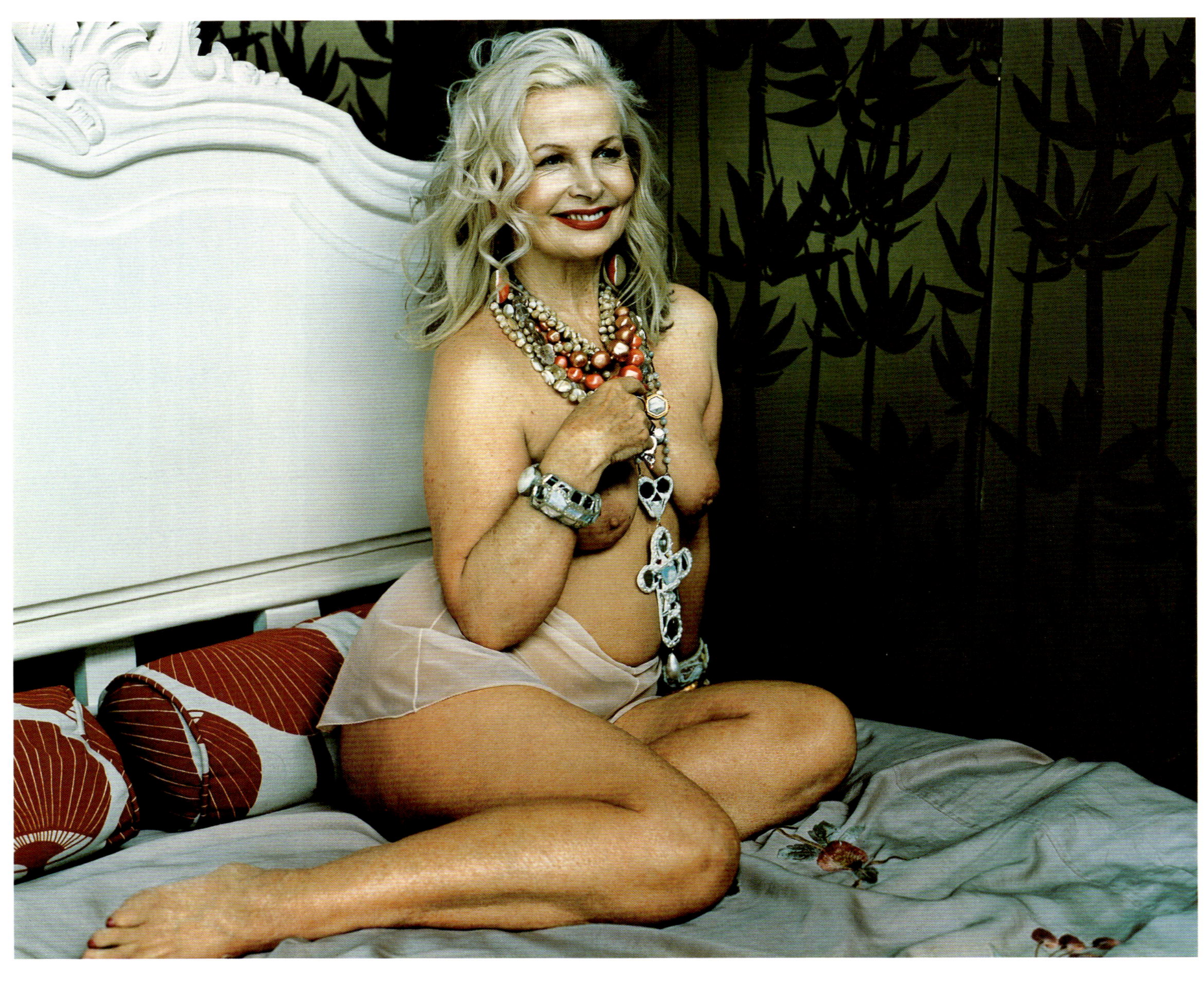

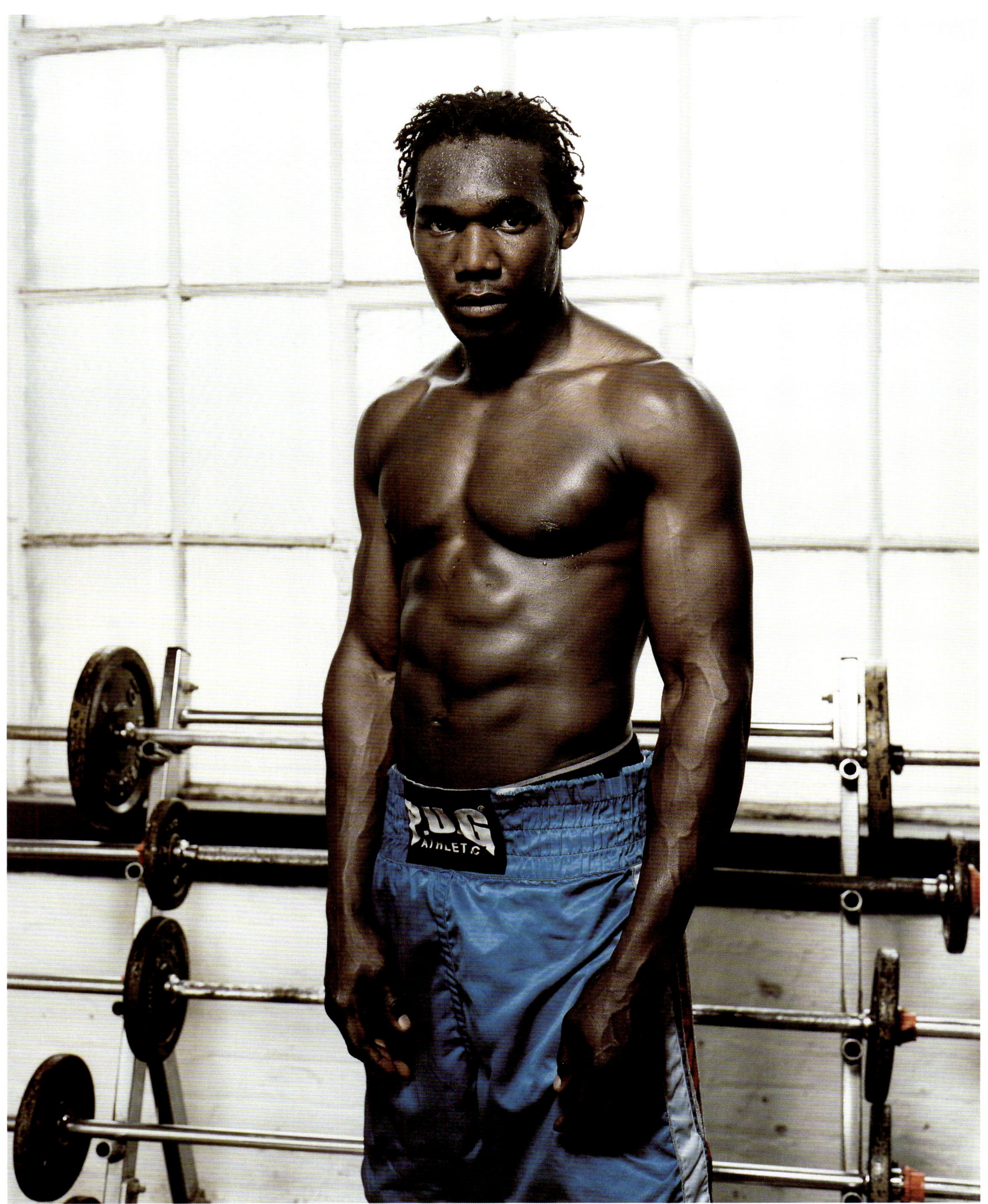

Morten Nilsson Untitled 7 *from the series* Dancers
April 2004

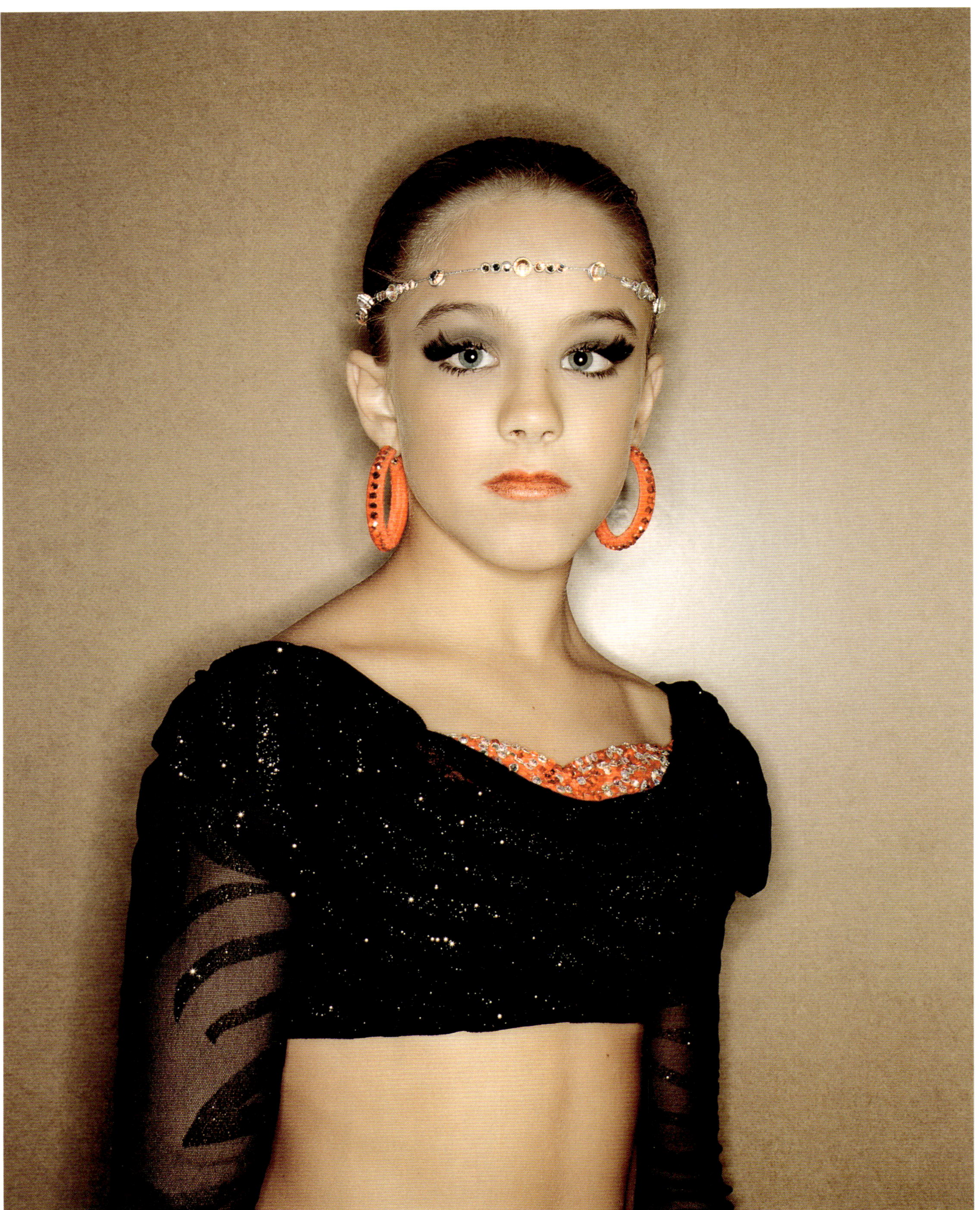

Susan Andrews Lois *from the series* Living in Harringay May 2004

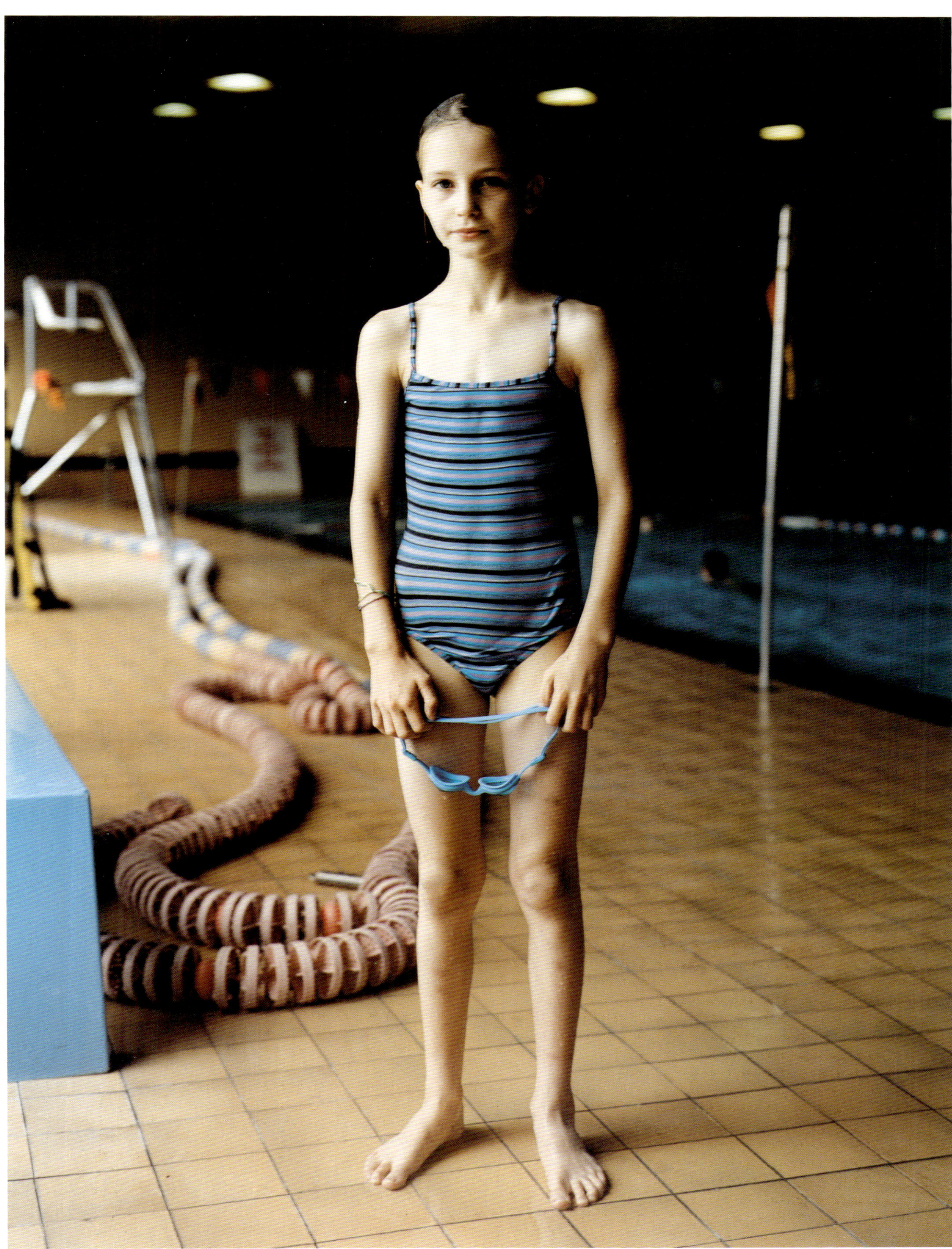

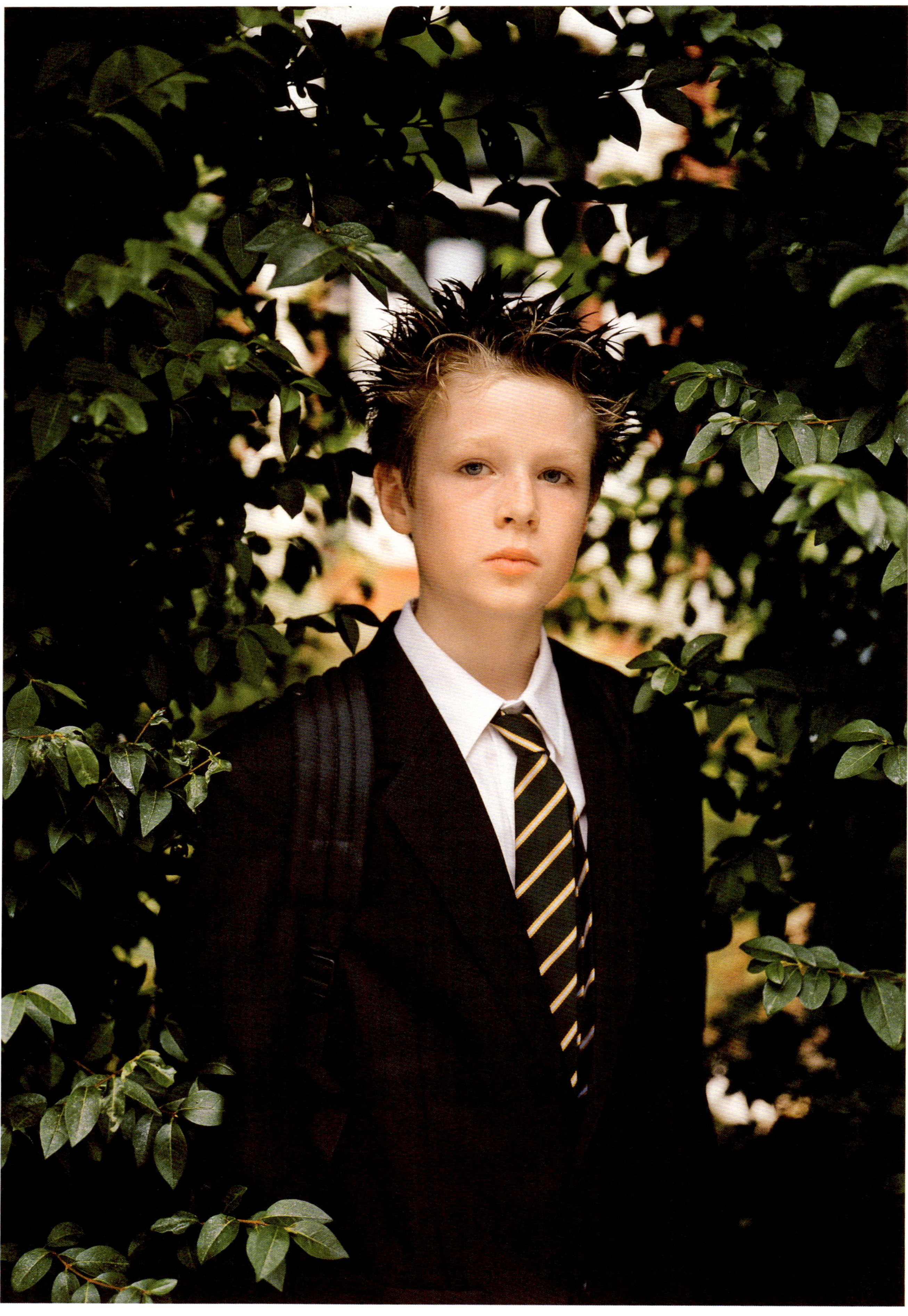

Opposite:
Seamus Ryan
Jack
July 2004

James
Yeats-Brown
The Catchpole
Family
November 2003

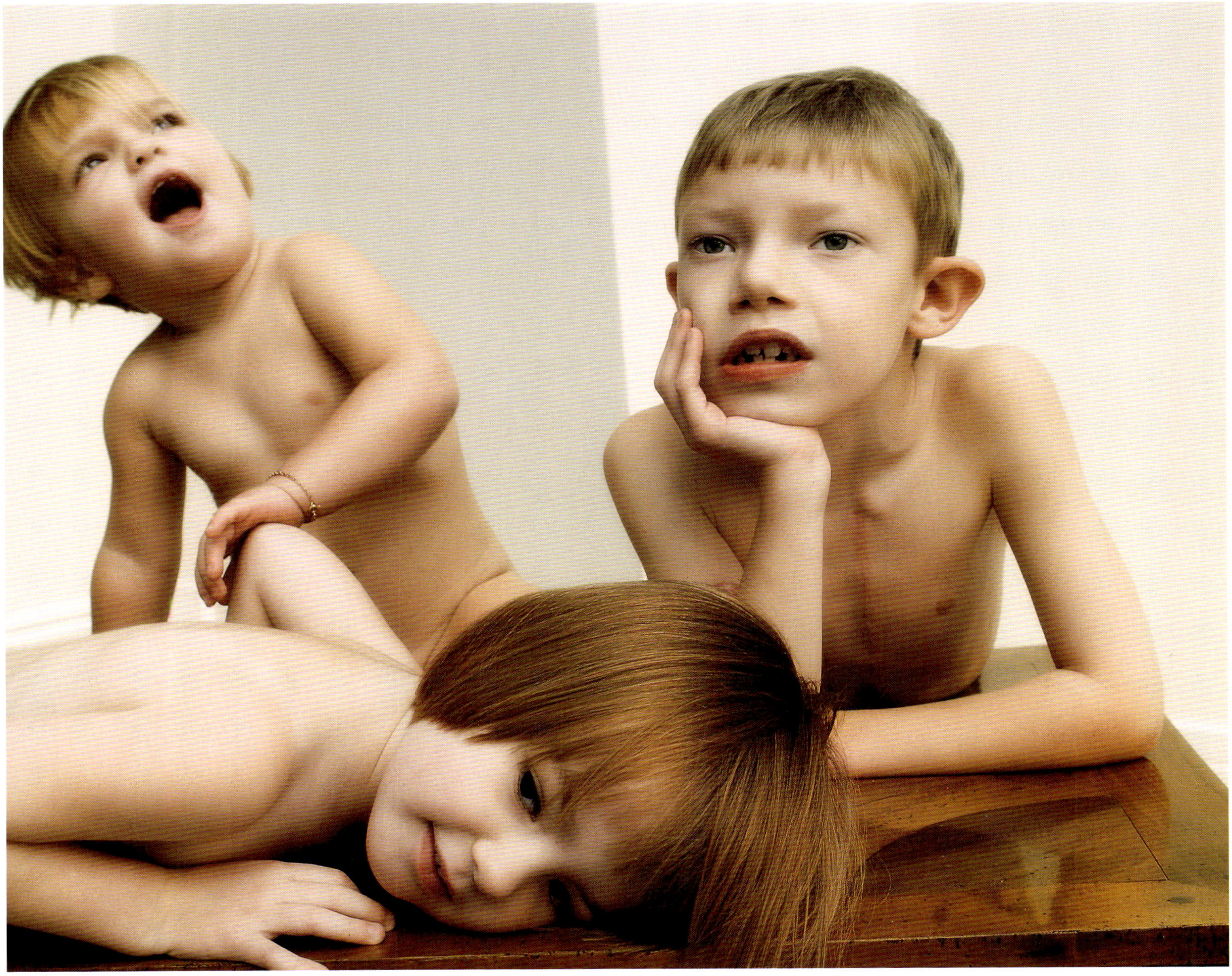

James Reeve

Sport – Afghanistan's 2004 Olympic Team
May 2004

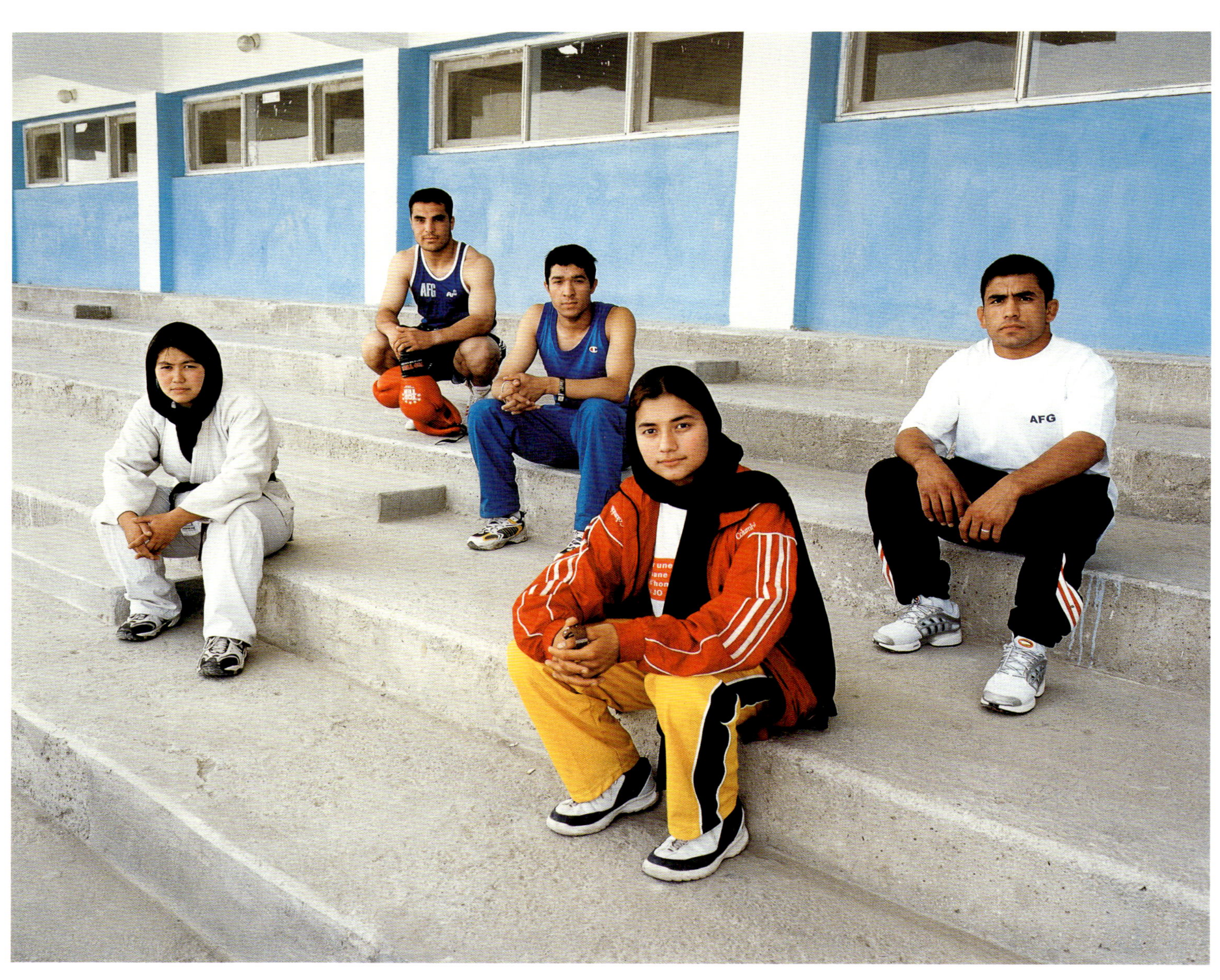

Dario Mitidieri

US Army Soldier
With Recovered
Gold Kalashnikov.
Saddam's
Presidential
Palace, Baghdad
April 2003

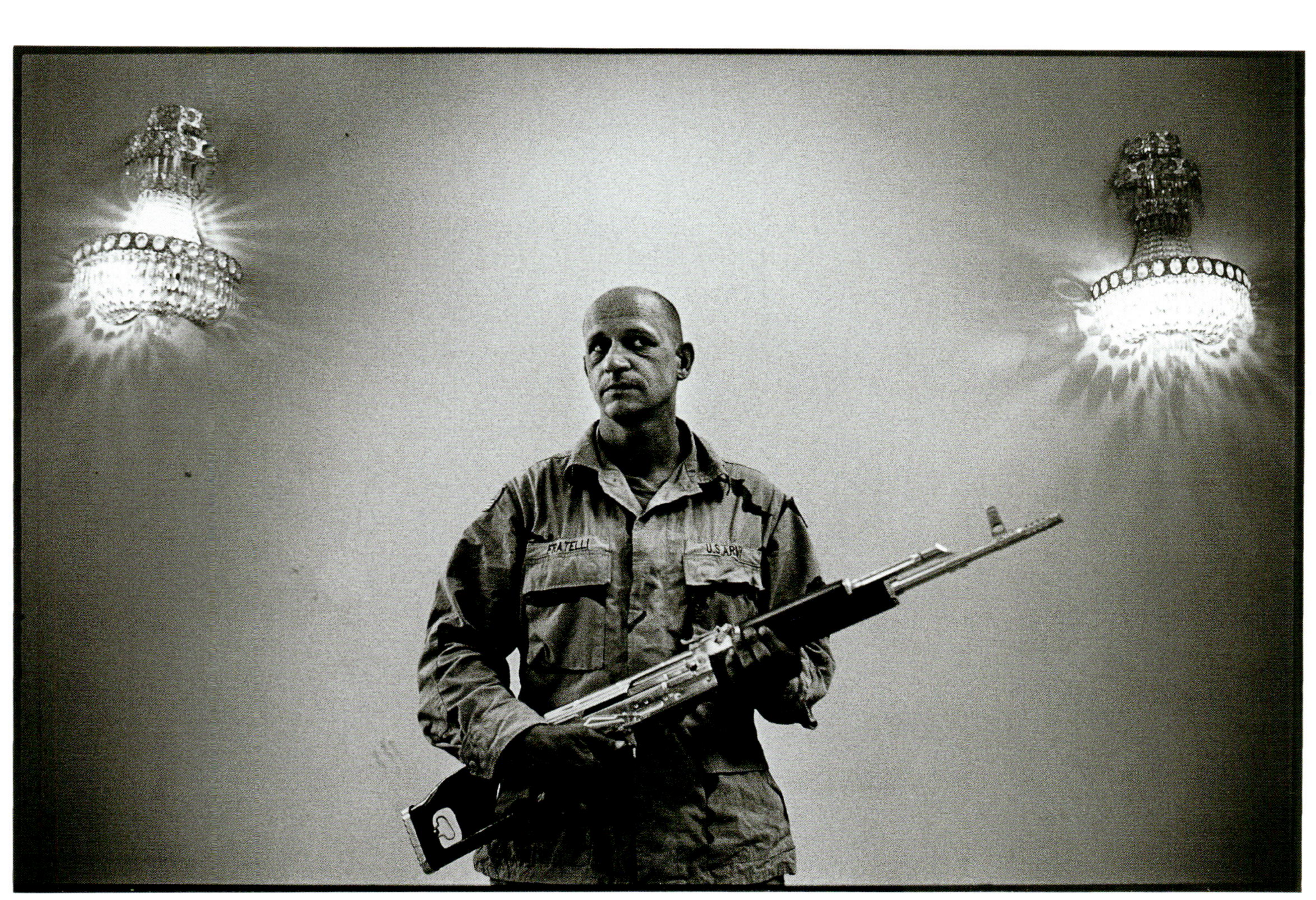

Lesley Anne Churchill

Xena
October 2003

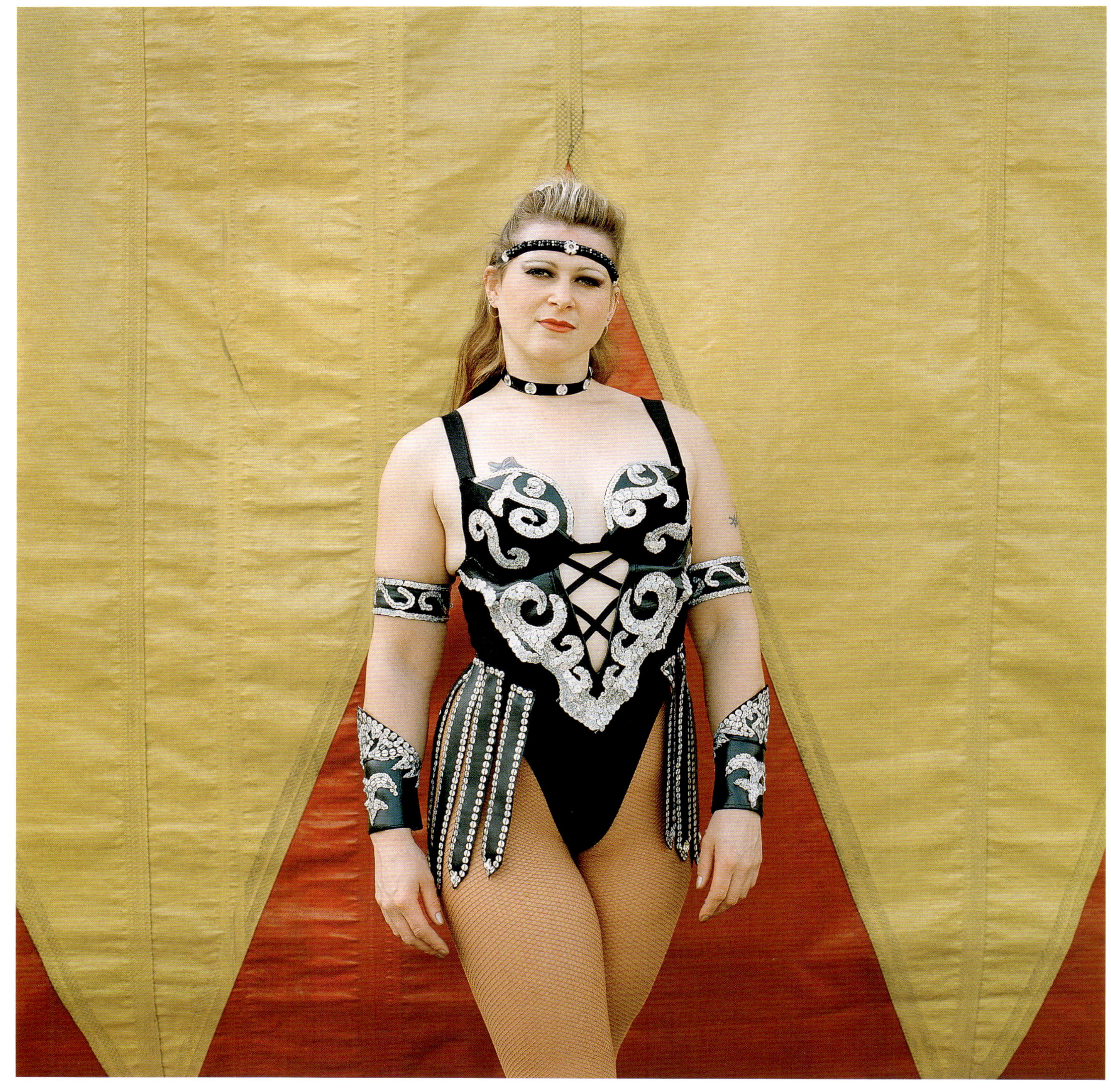

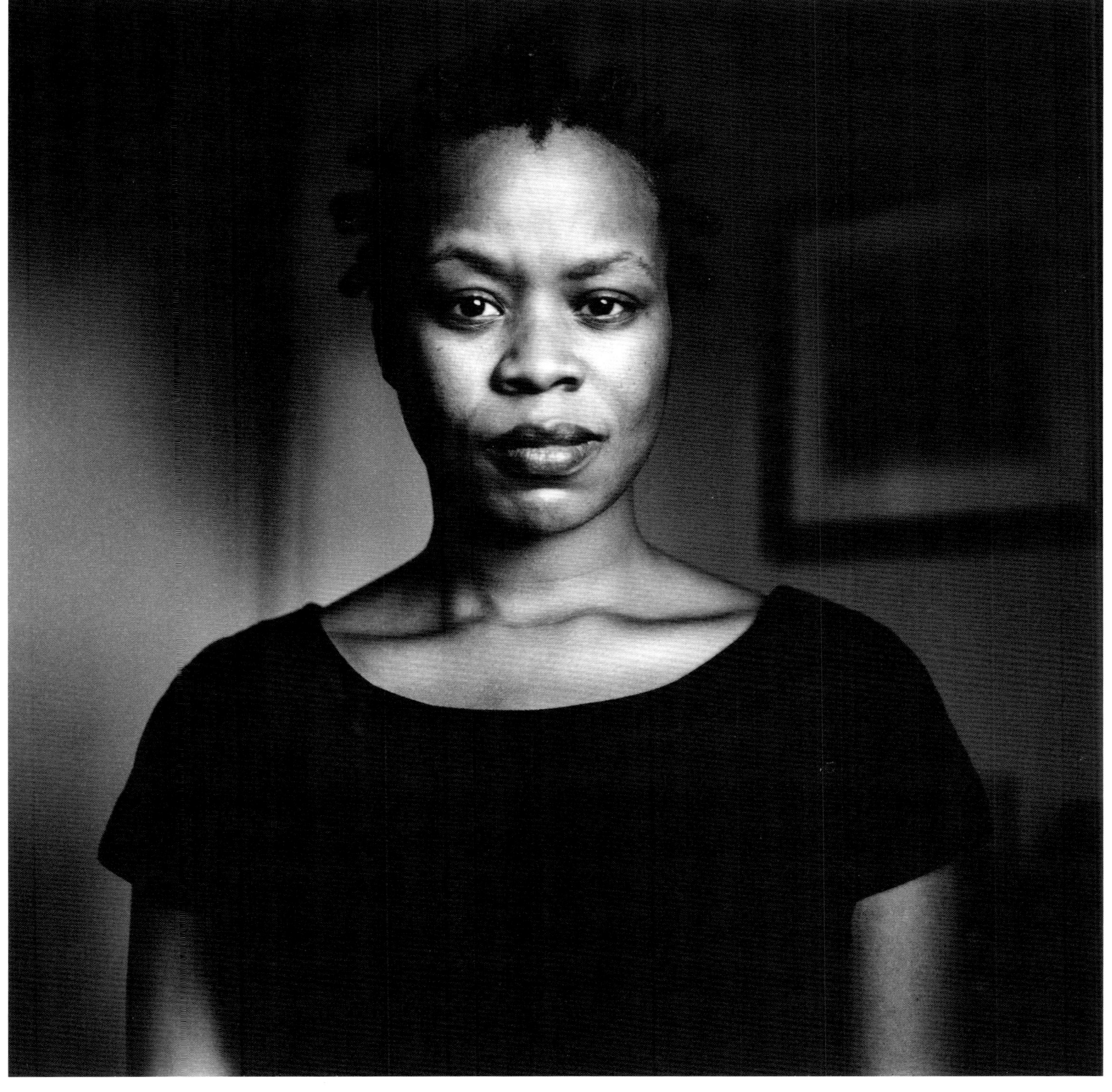

Zoltán Jókay

Untitled *from the series* Strange

October 2003

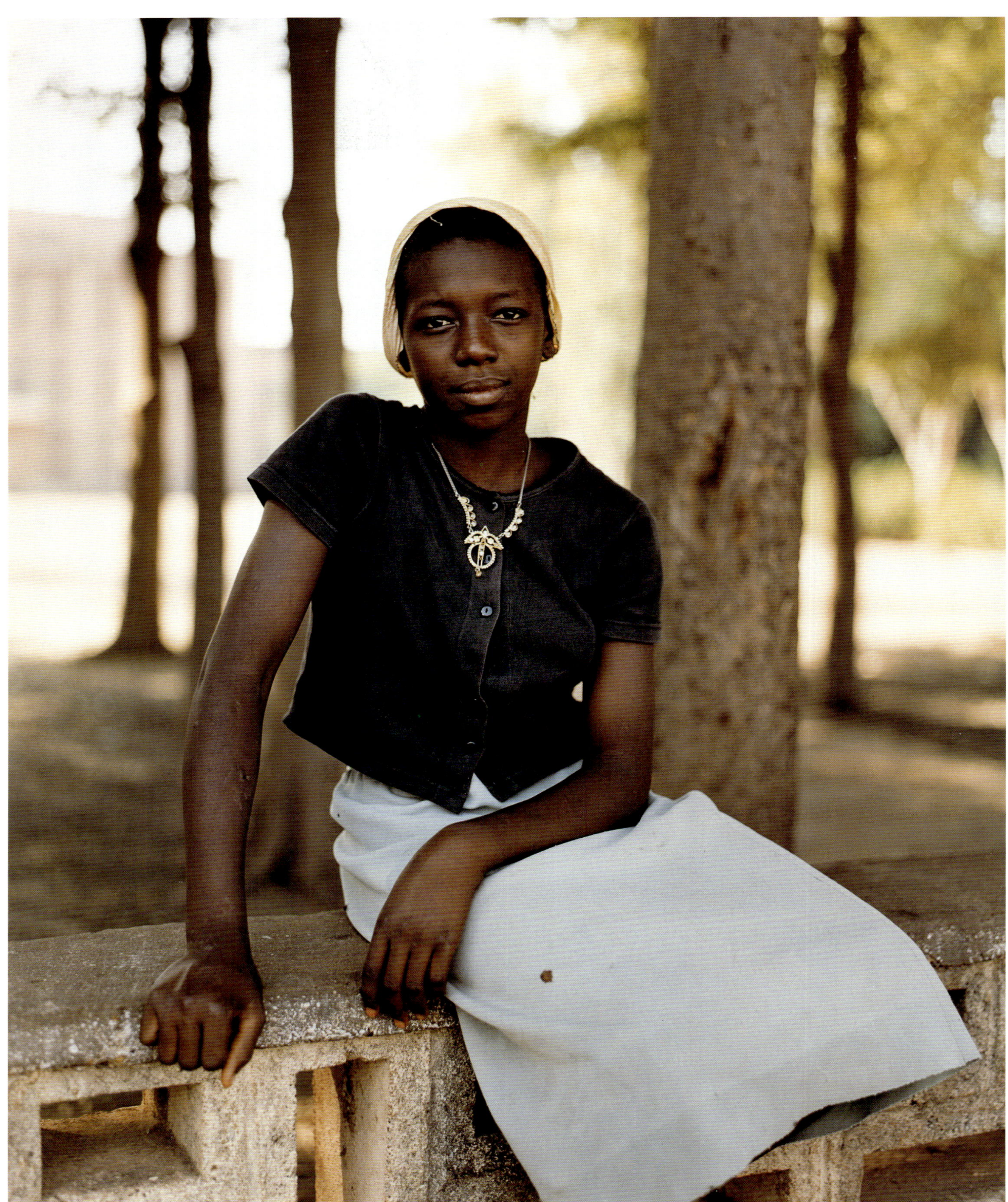

Carlos Villanueva Brandt

Henrietta With Her Hair Down *from the series* Henrietta in the Studio
July 2003

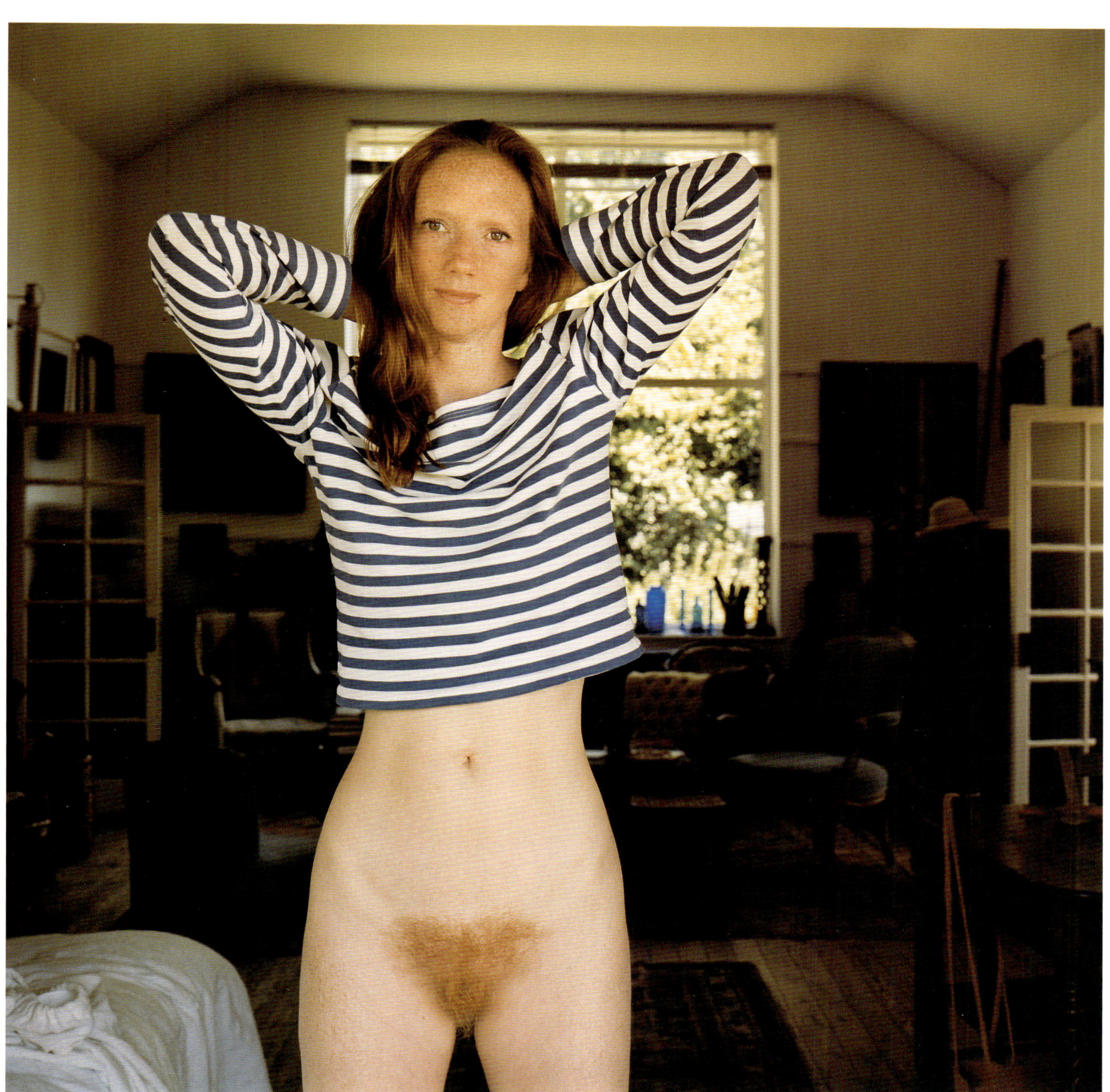

Michal Chelbin

'Grandfather', Russia, 2003 *from the series* Private Visits January 2003

Opposite: Beso Uznadze

Patriot *from the series* A Hero For Our Time October 2003

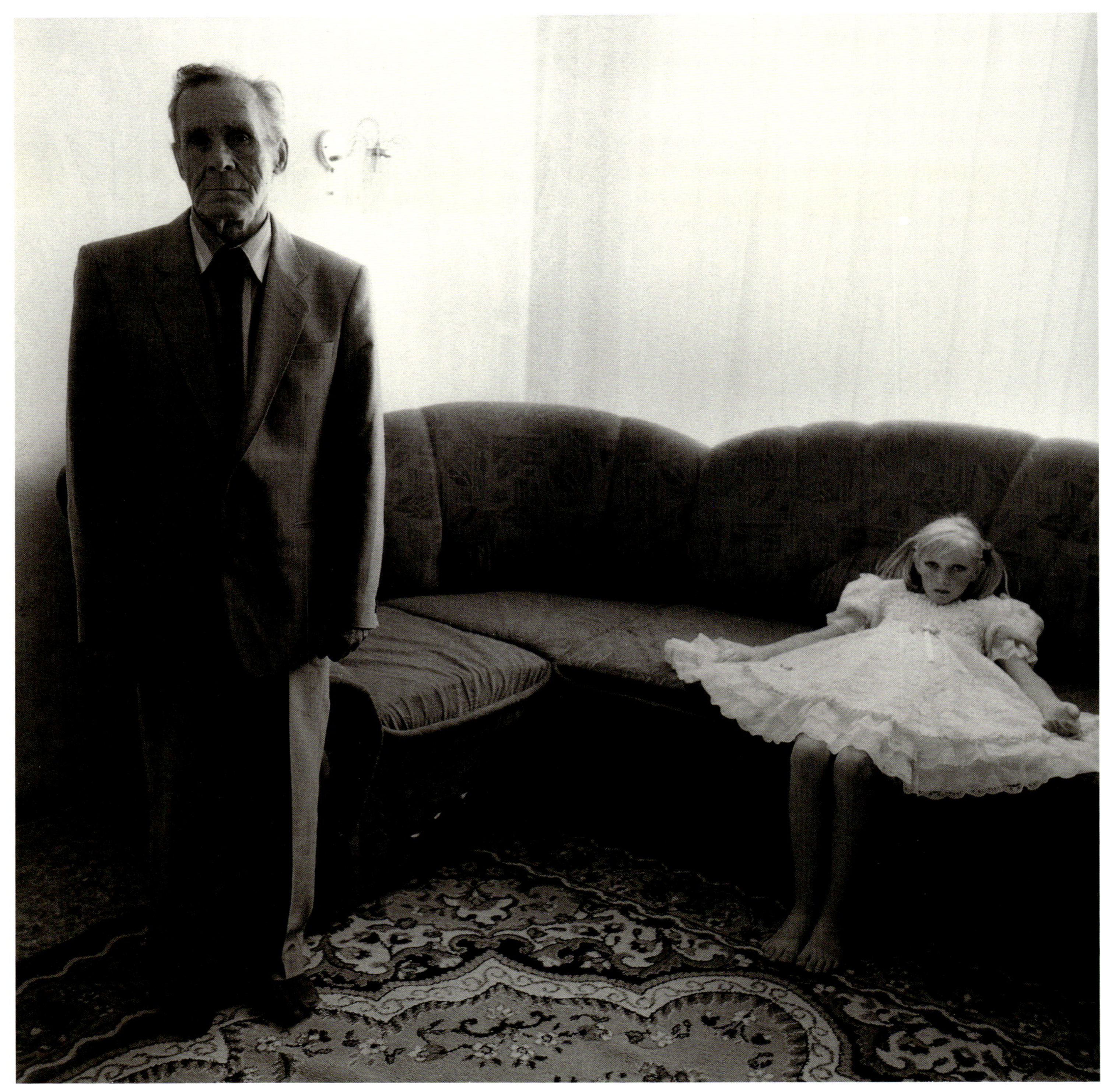

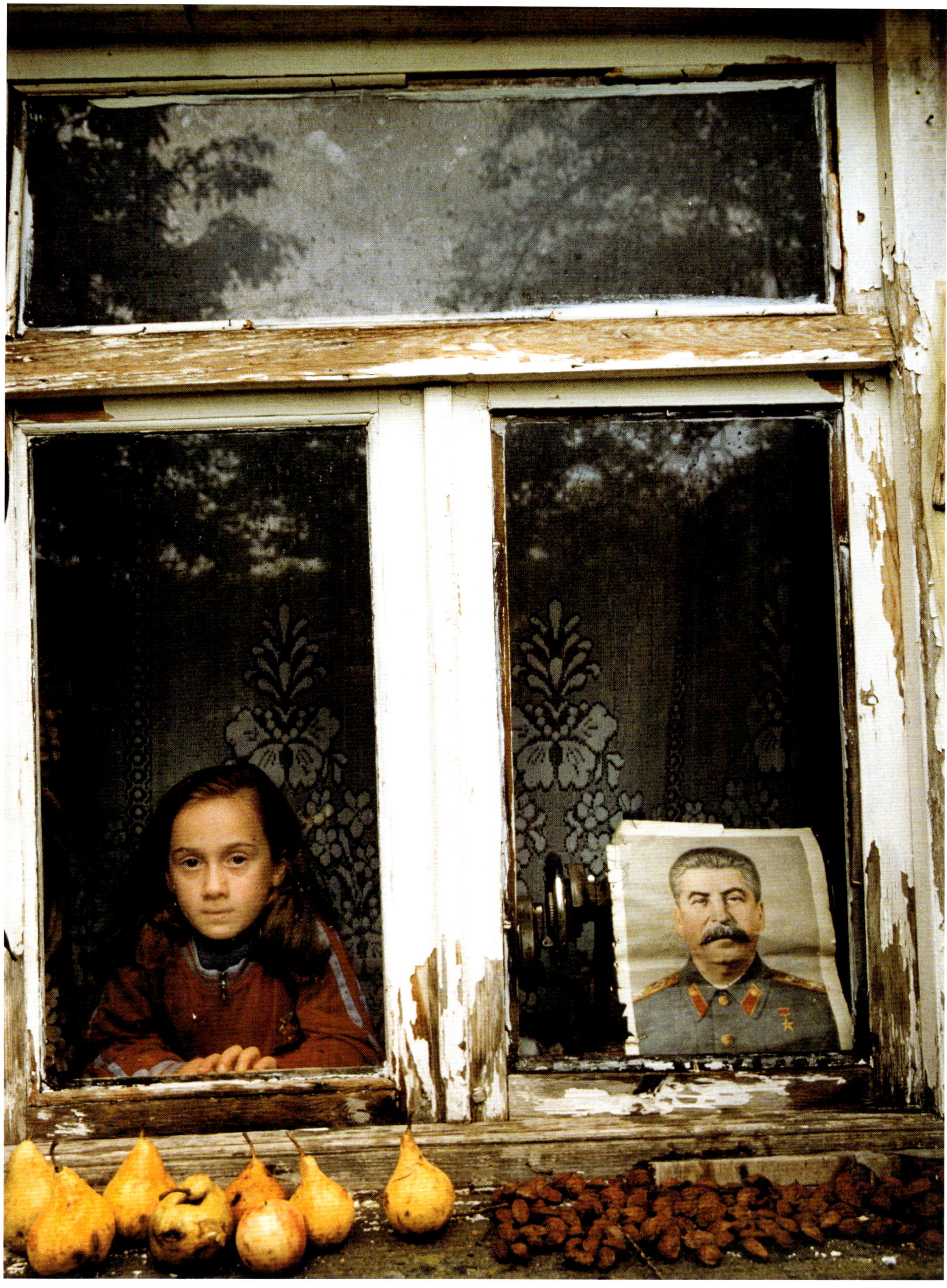

Zed Nelson

Debbie Demayl
October 2003

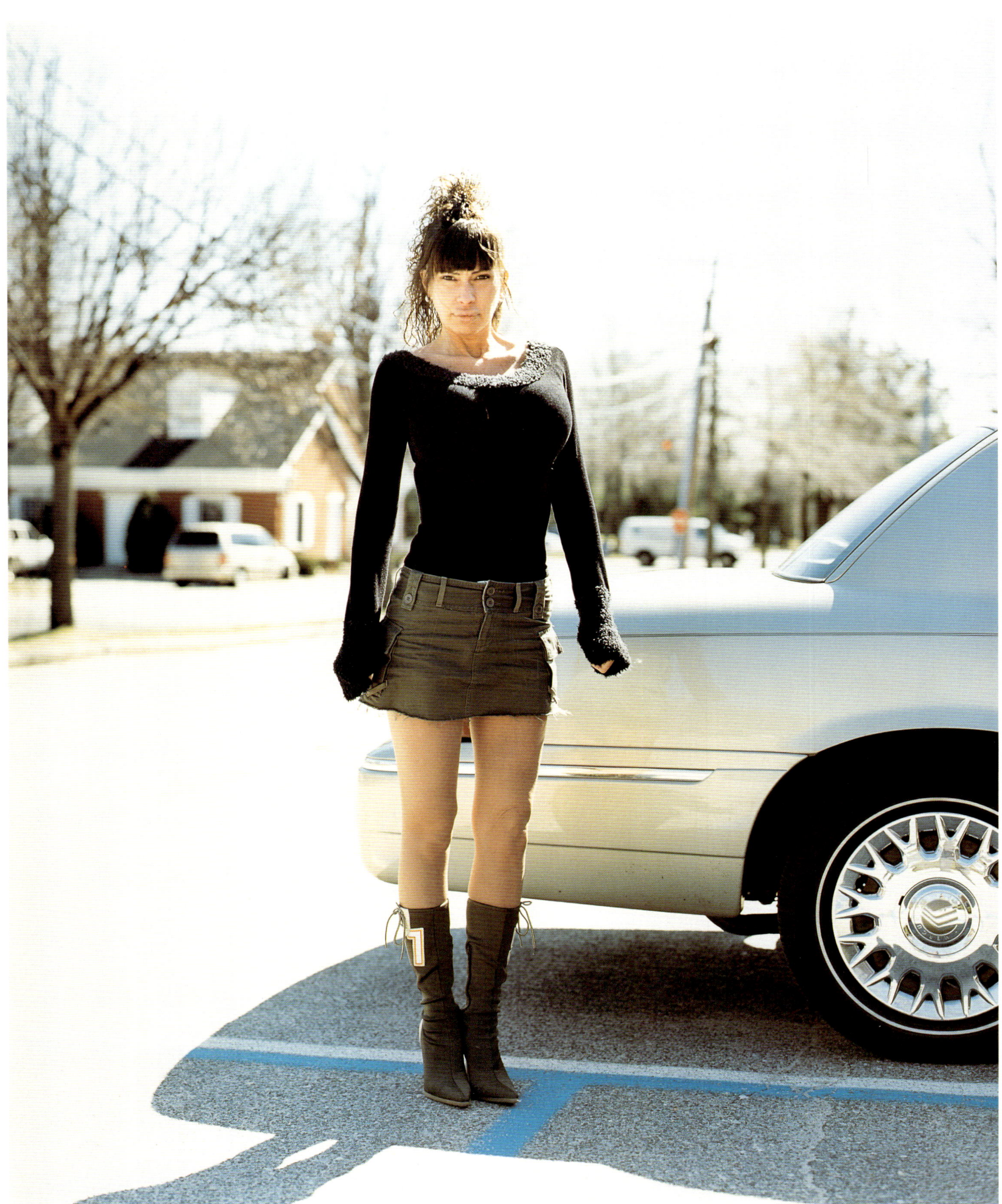

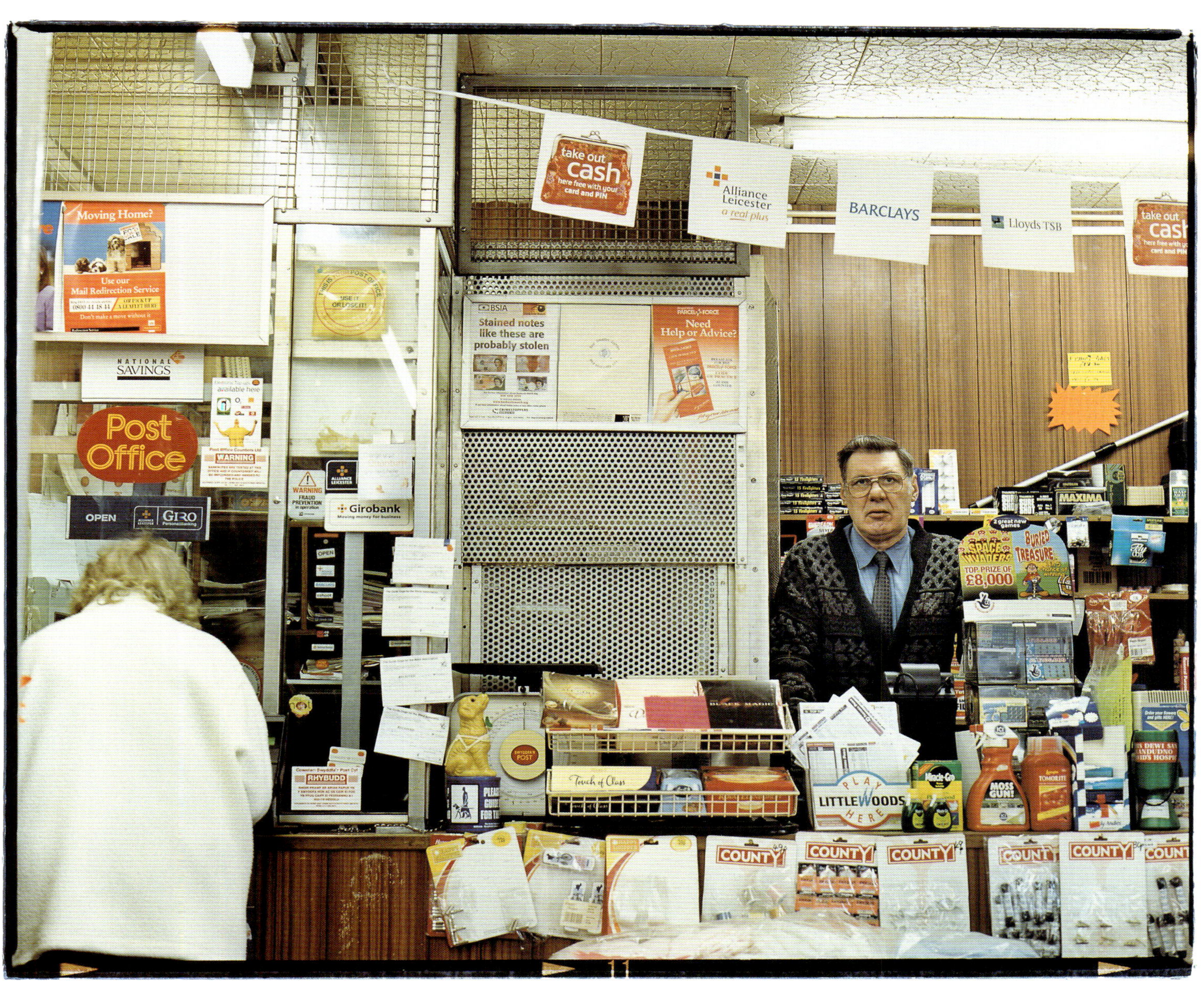
take out cash
here free with your card and PIN
Alliance Leicester
a real plus
BARCLAYS
Lloyds TSB
Moving Home?
Use our Mail Redirection Service
NATIONAL SAVINGS
Post Office
OPEN
GIRO
Stained notes like these are probably stolen
Need Help or Advice?
WARNING
Girobank
RHYBUDD
Touch of Class
LITTLEWOODS
PLAY HERE
TOP PRIZE OF £8,000
BURIED TREASURE
MOSS GUN!
COUNTY
MAXIMA

Konstantin
June 2003

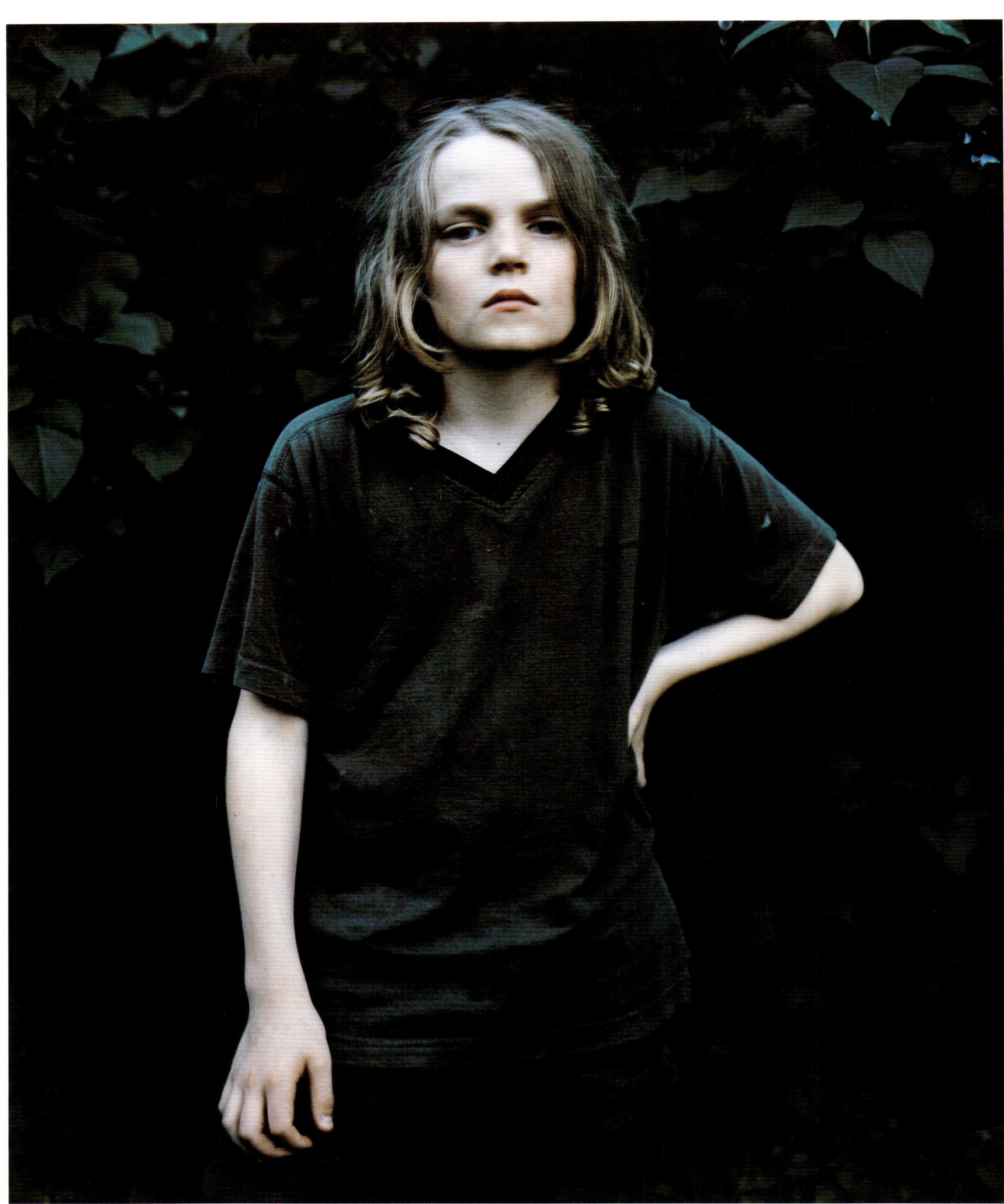

Jessica Backhaus

Olga *from the series* Poland
August 2003

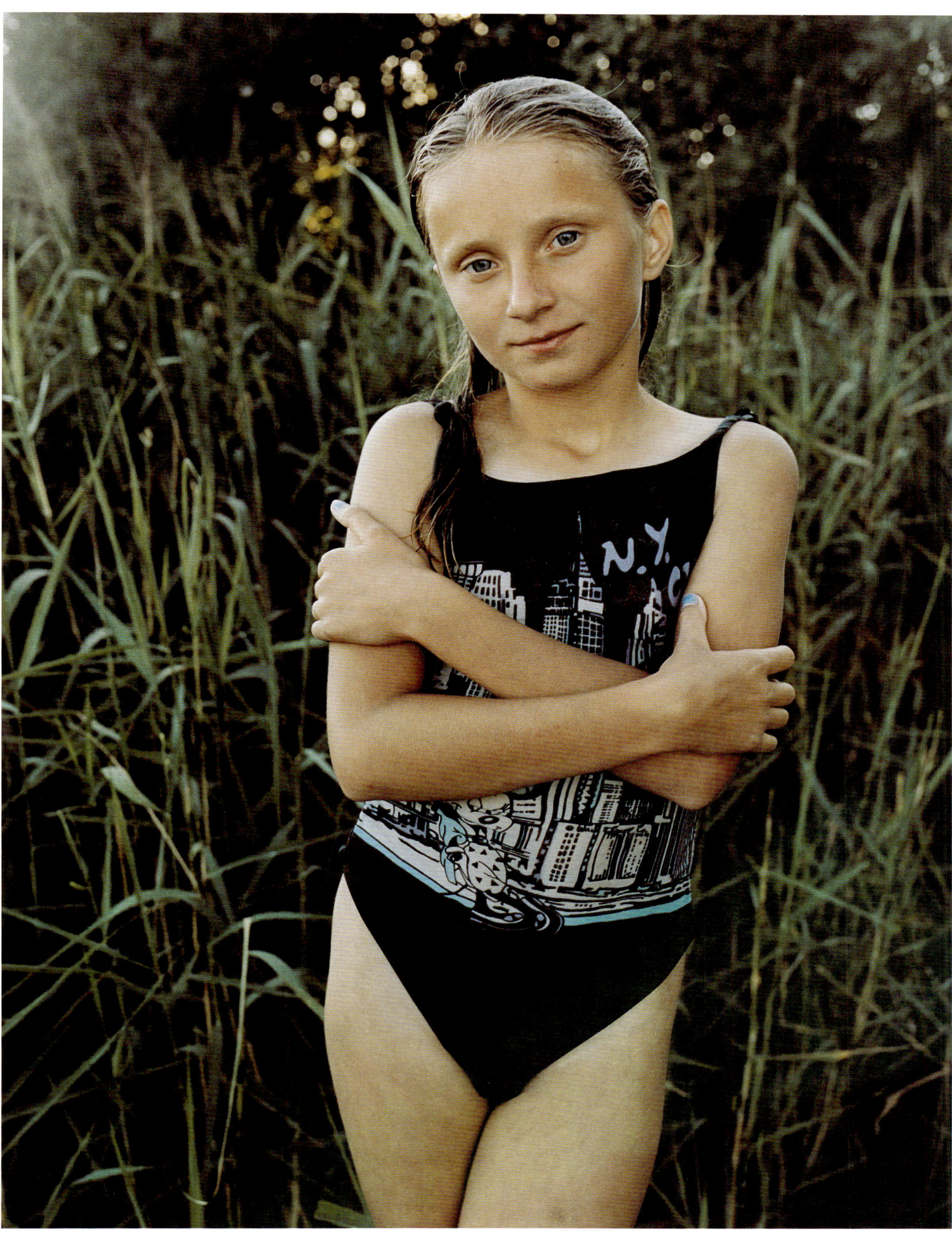

Julia Fullerton-Batten

Shanghai Subway
May 2004

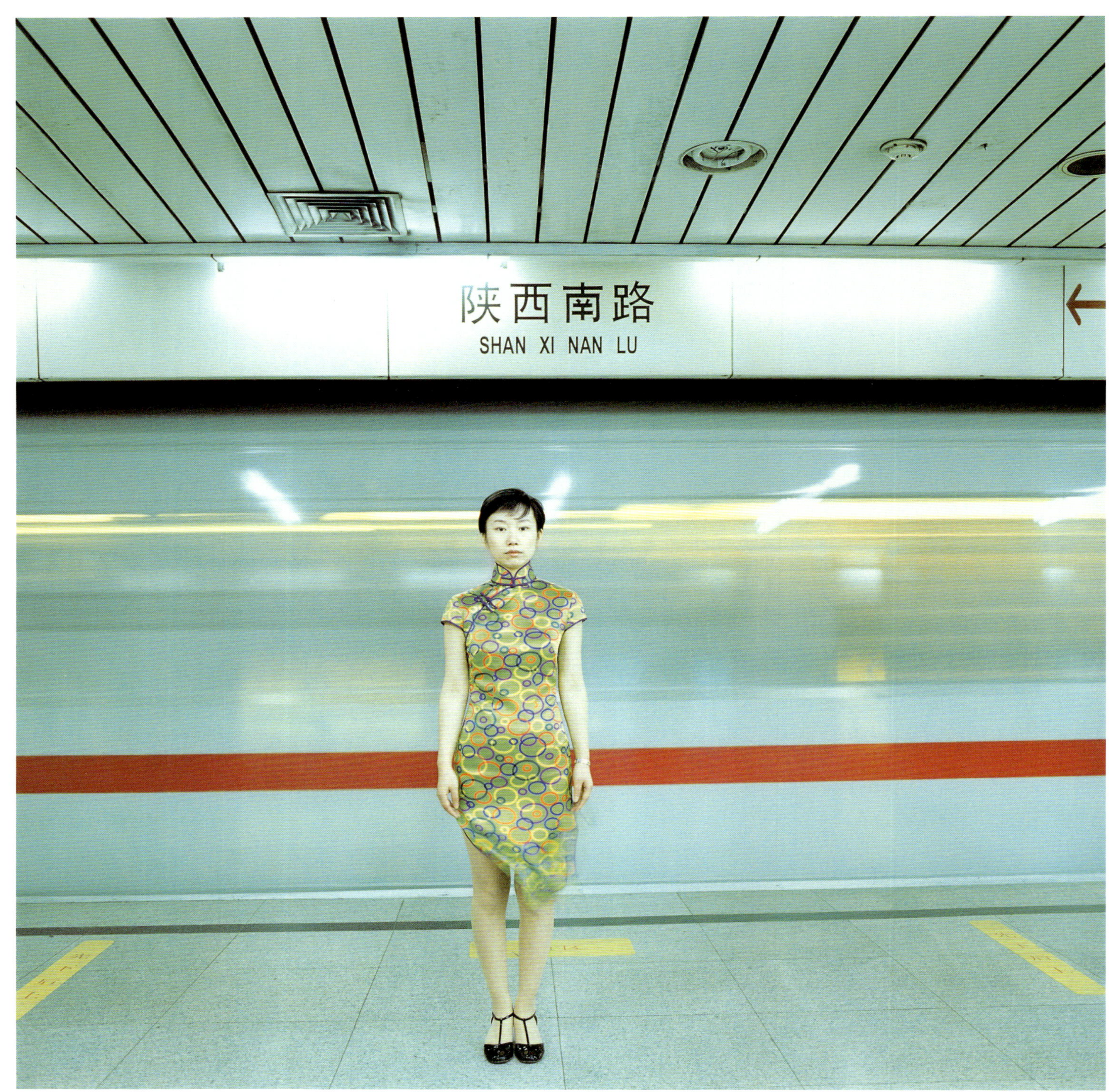

Robin George Stanley

Waiting *from the series* The Perimeter
May 2004

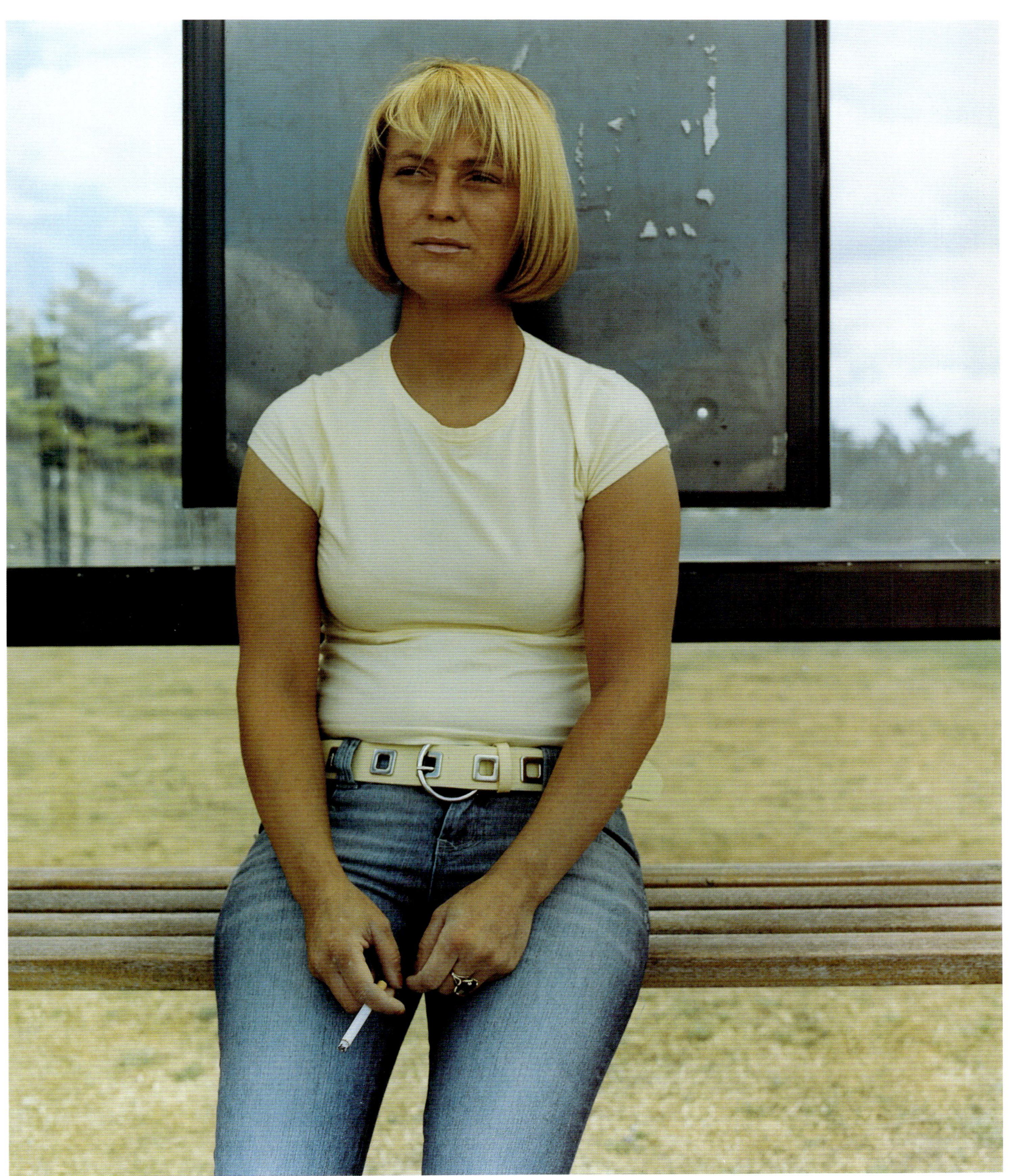

Rory Carnegie Amina
February 2004

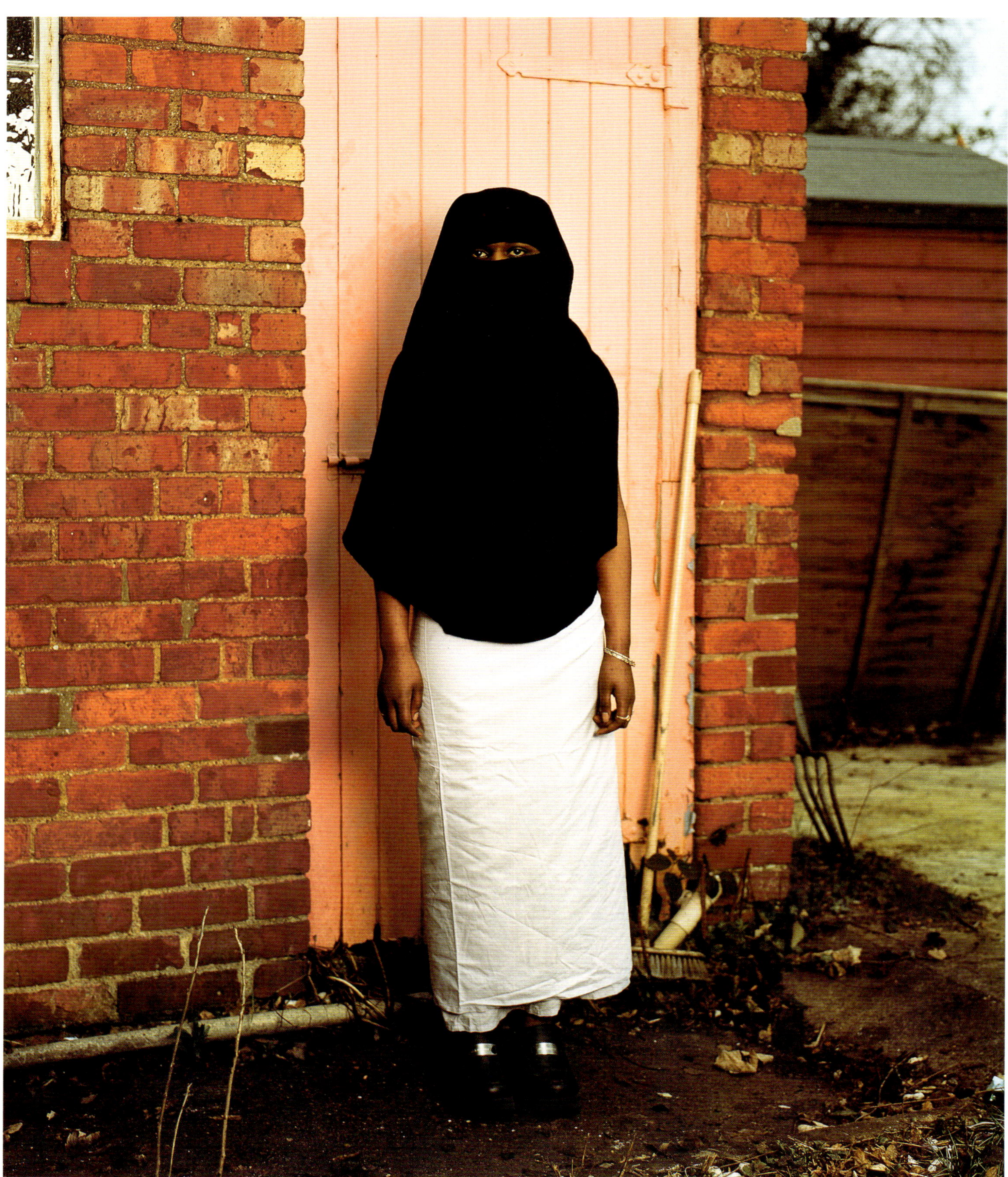

Allan F. Parker

Family Group on Mahashivaratri Holiday, Lalbagh Gardens, Bangalore
February 2004

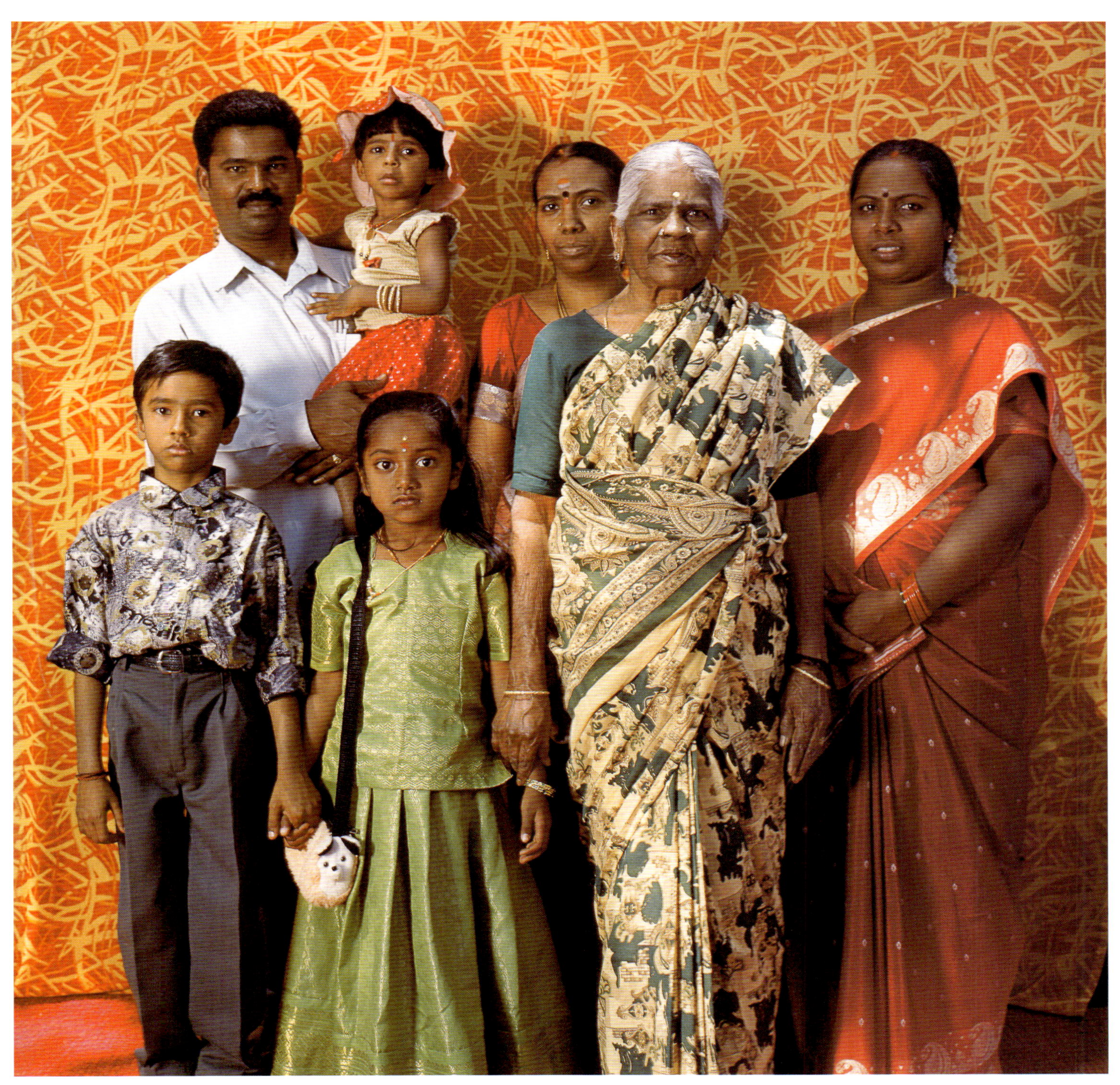

Paul Blake

George, Church of the New Testament of God, Halifax *from the series* The Changing Face of Yorkshire December 2003

Opposite: Tom Craig

One Day I'm Going to be President of South Africa February 2003

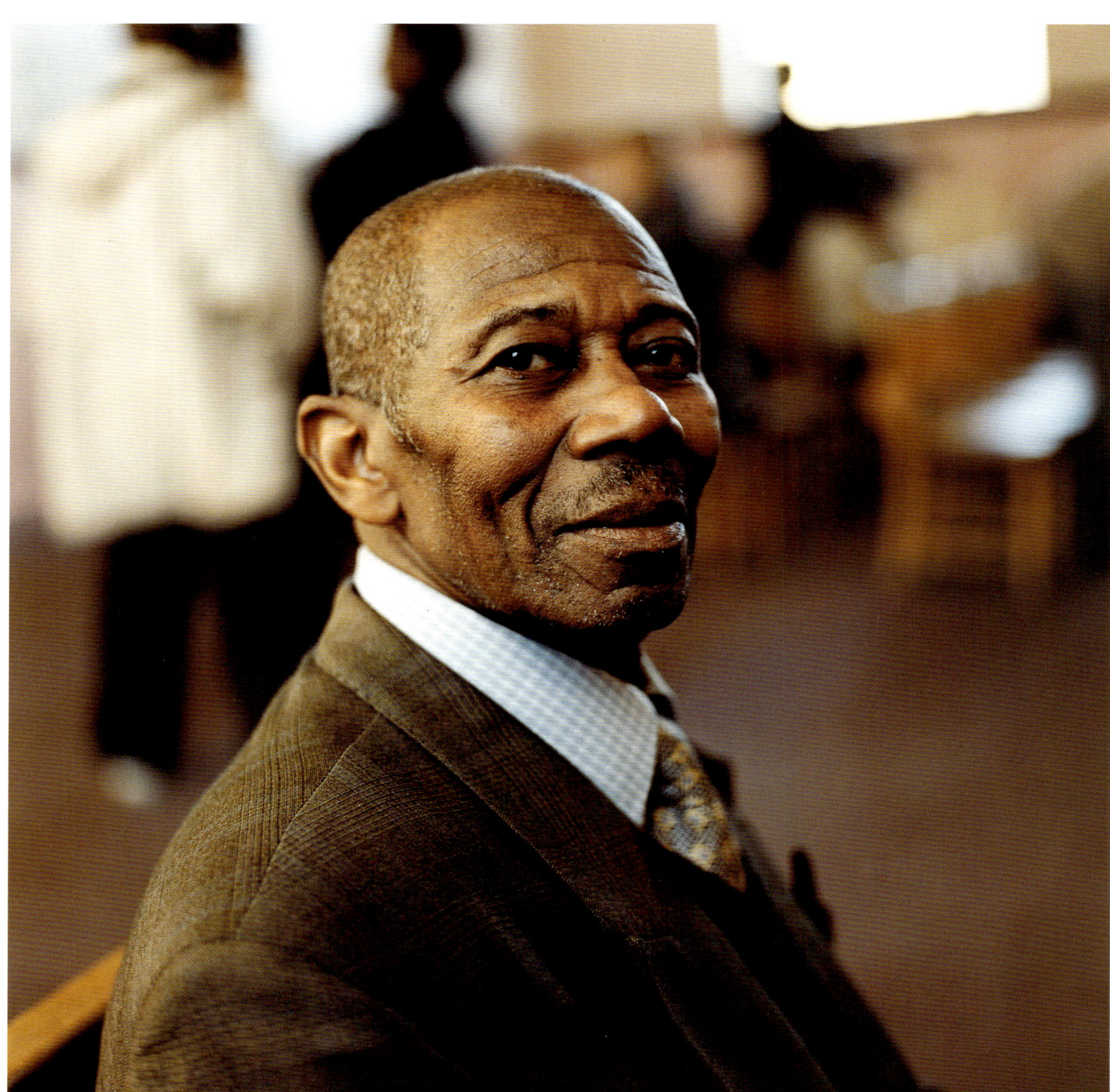

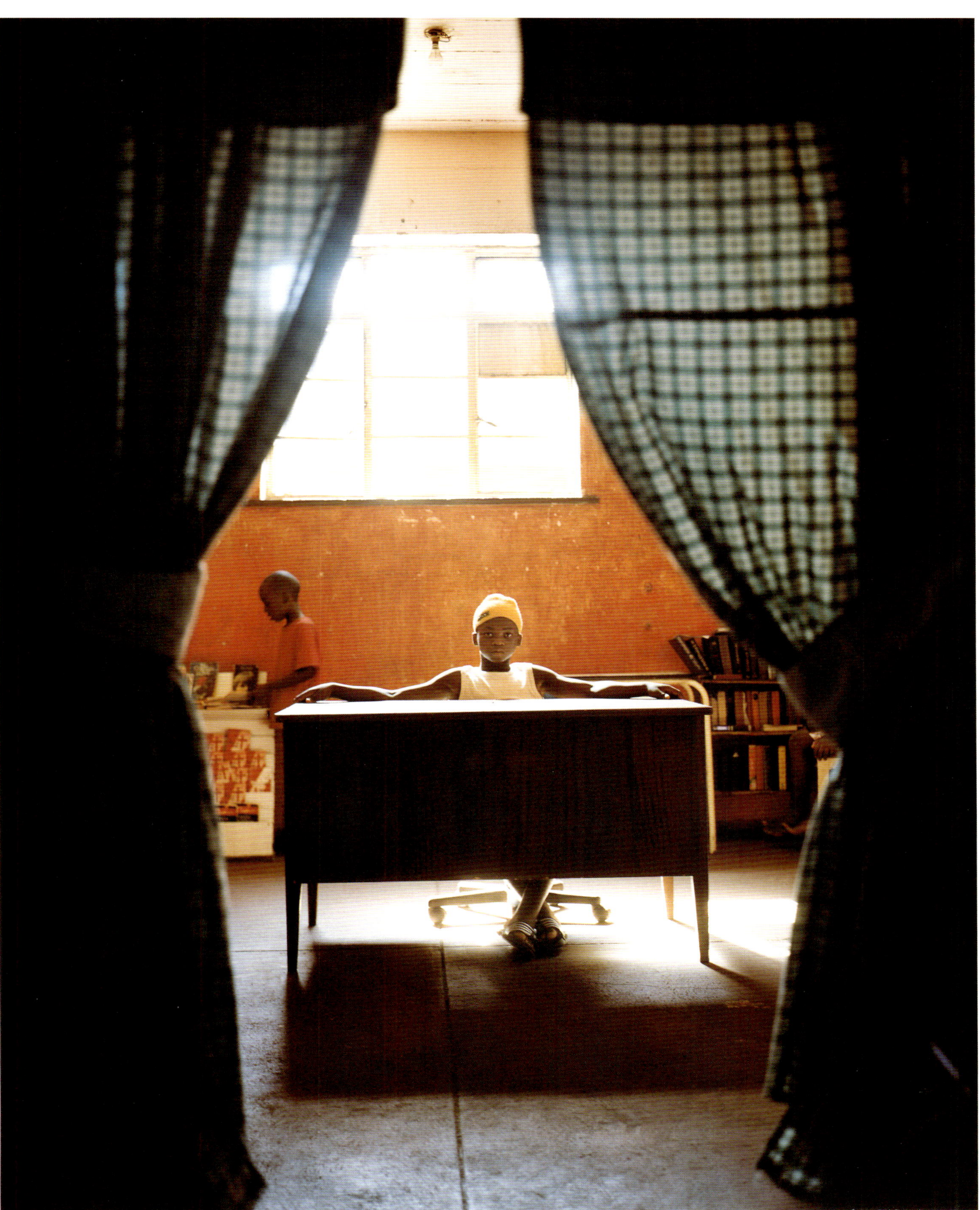

Claire Waffel

Untitled *from the series* Close Family
July 2003

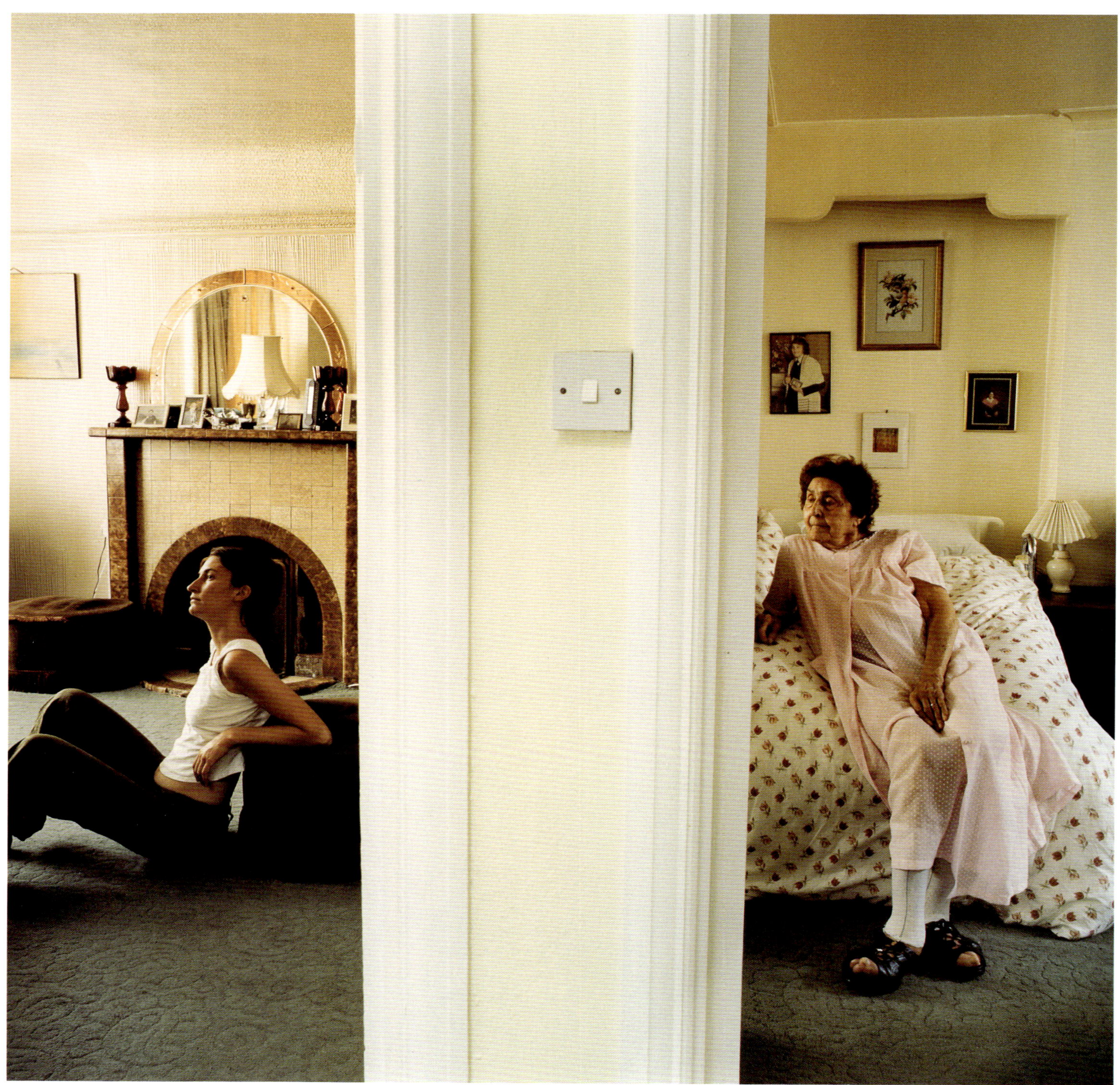

Paul Thompson | *Happy Families* from the series | Families | June 2004

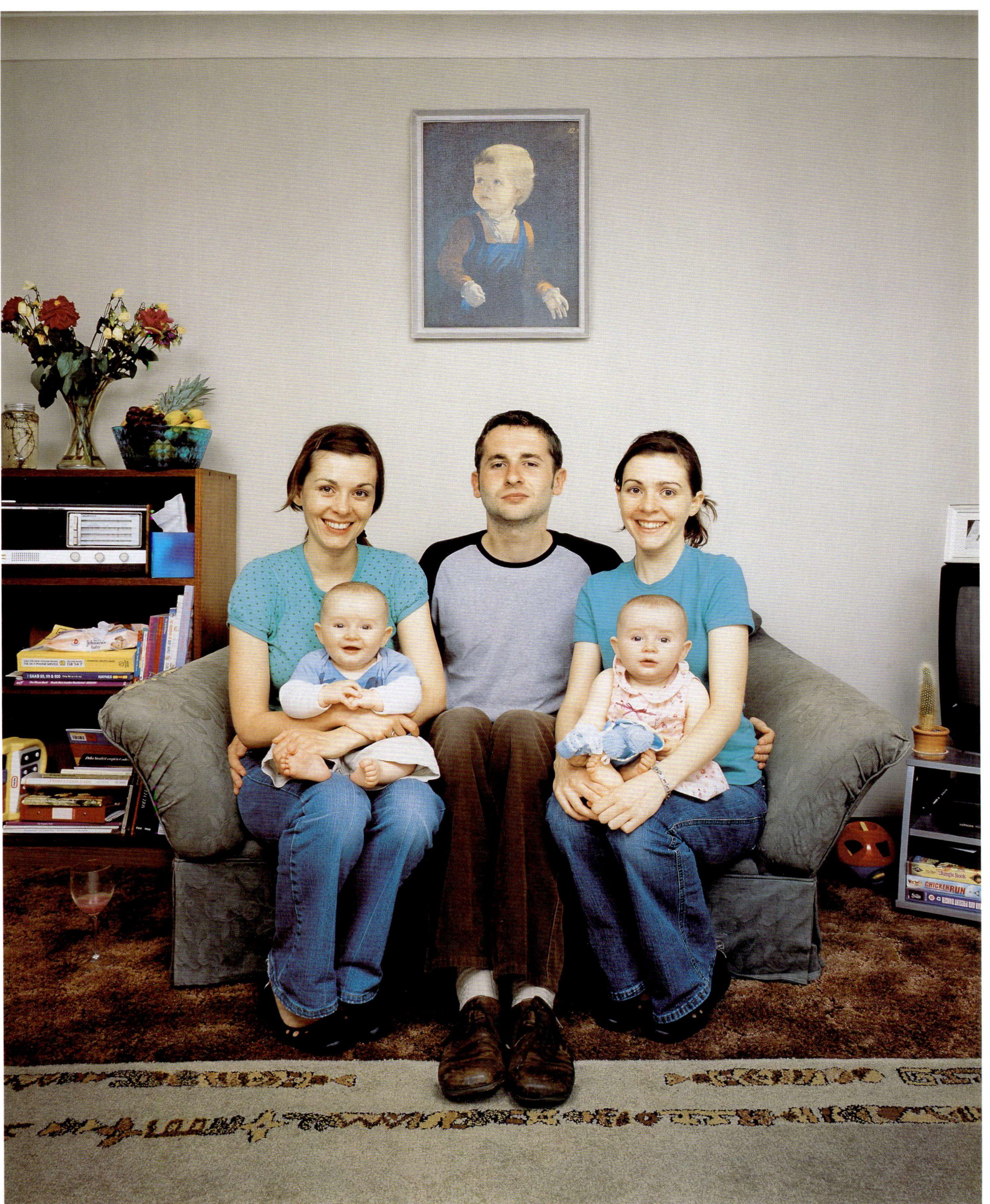

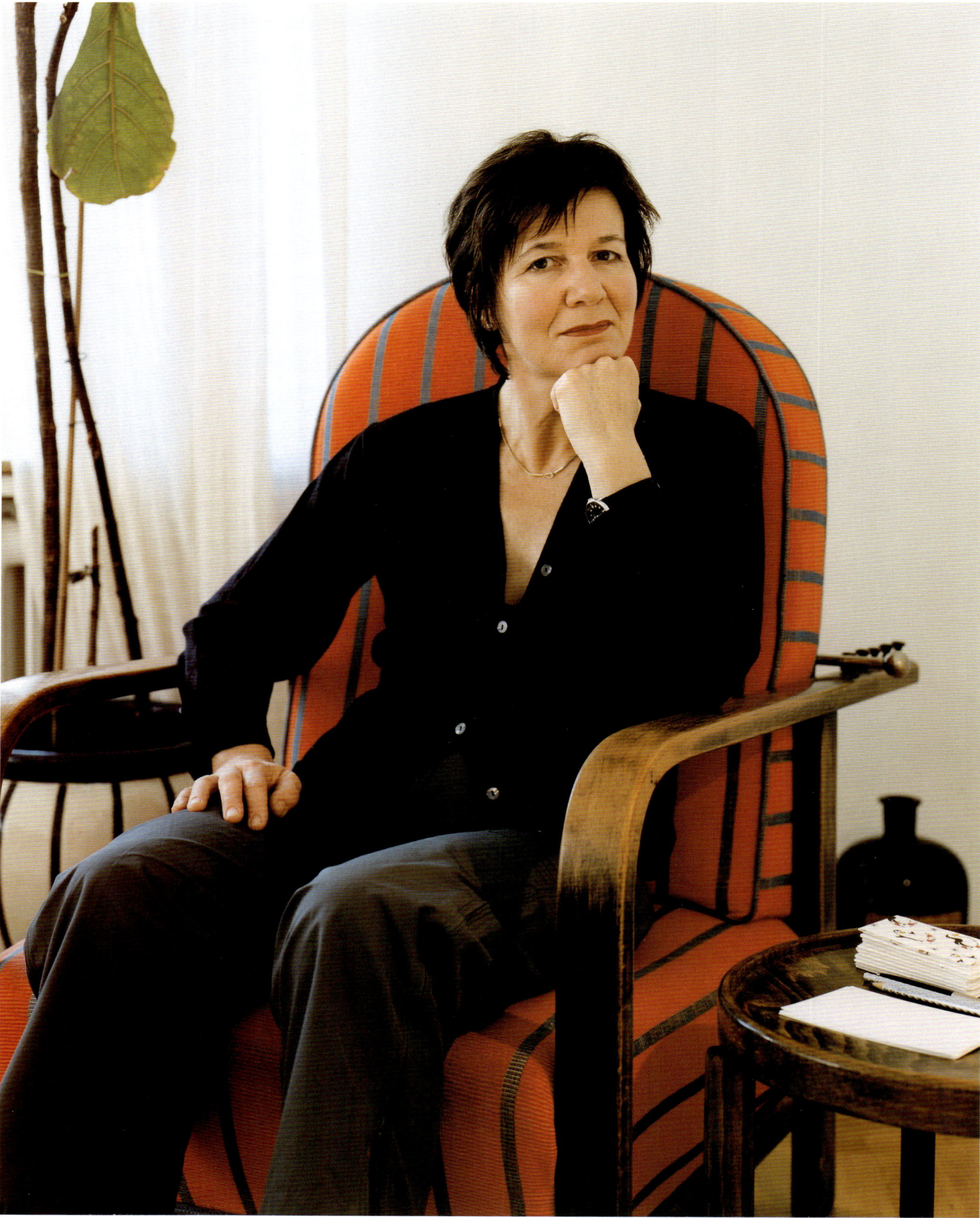

Markus Haefke

Nancy and Christopher
May 2003

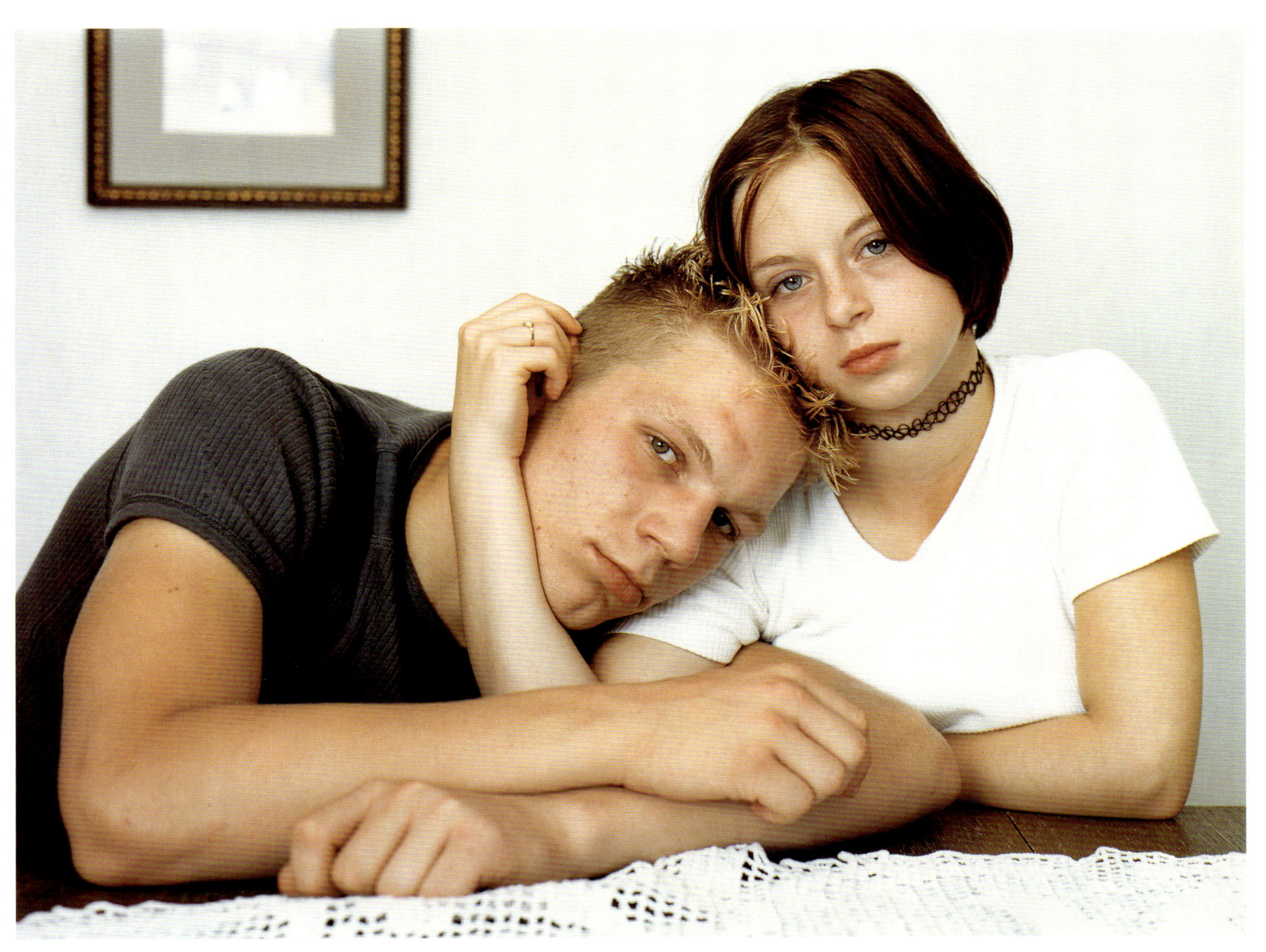

Hugo Tillman

Mrs Edwin Burke
from the series
Upper Class
June 2004

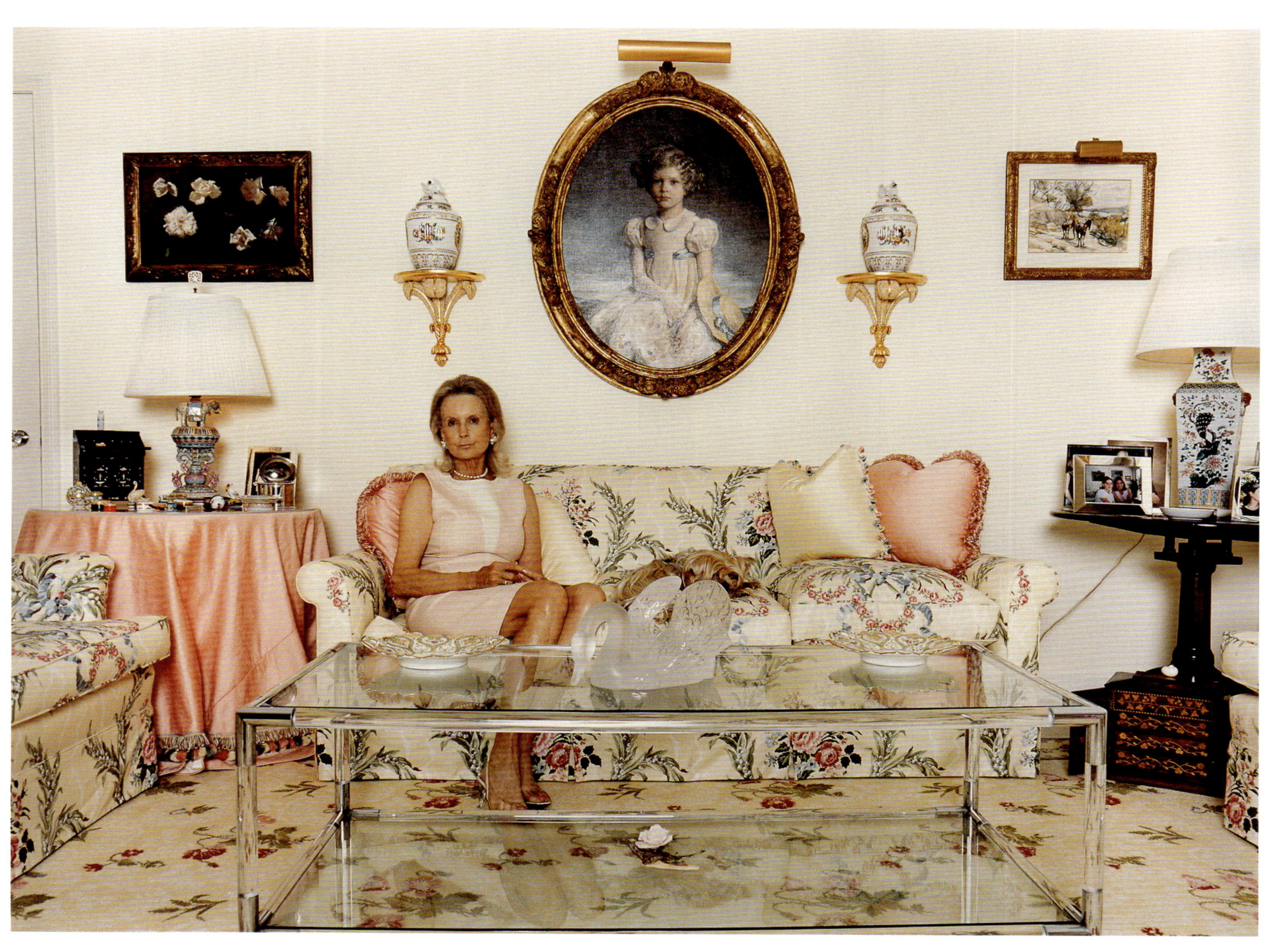

Pernille Koldbech Fich

Carla *from the series* Sisters
May 2003

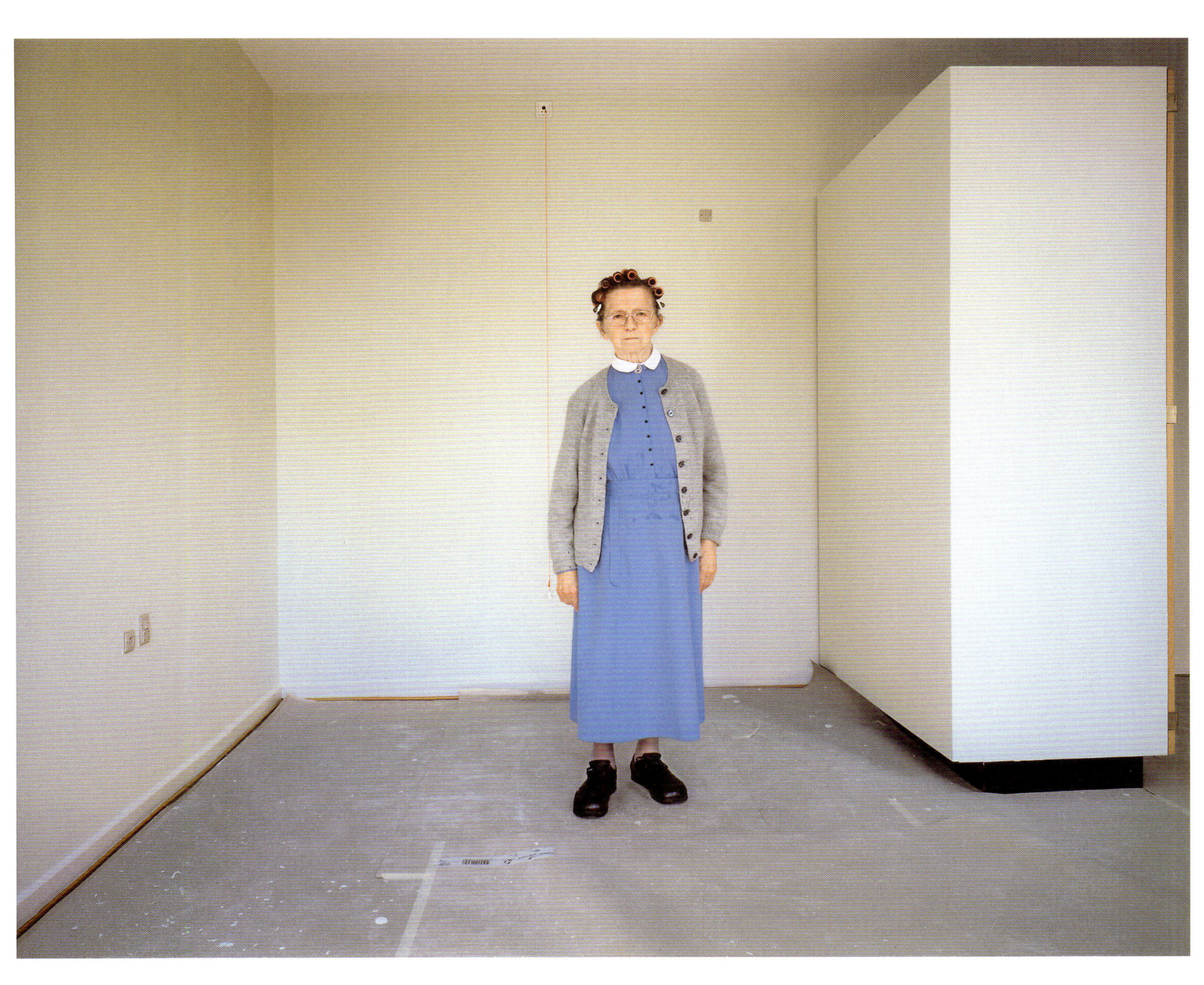

Tara Moore

Leabank Square 2 *from the series* Leabank Square
June 2004

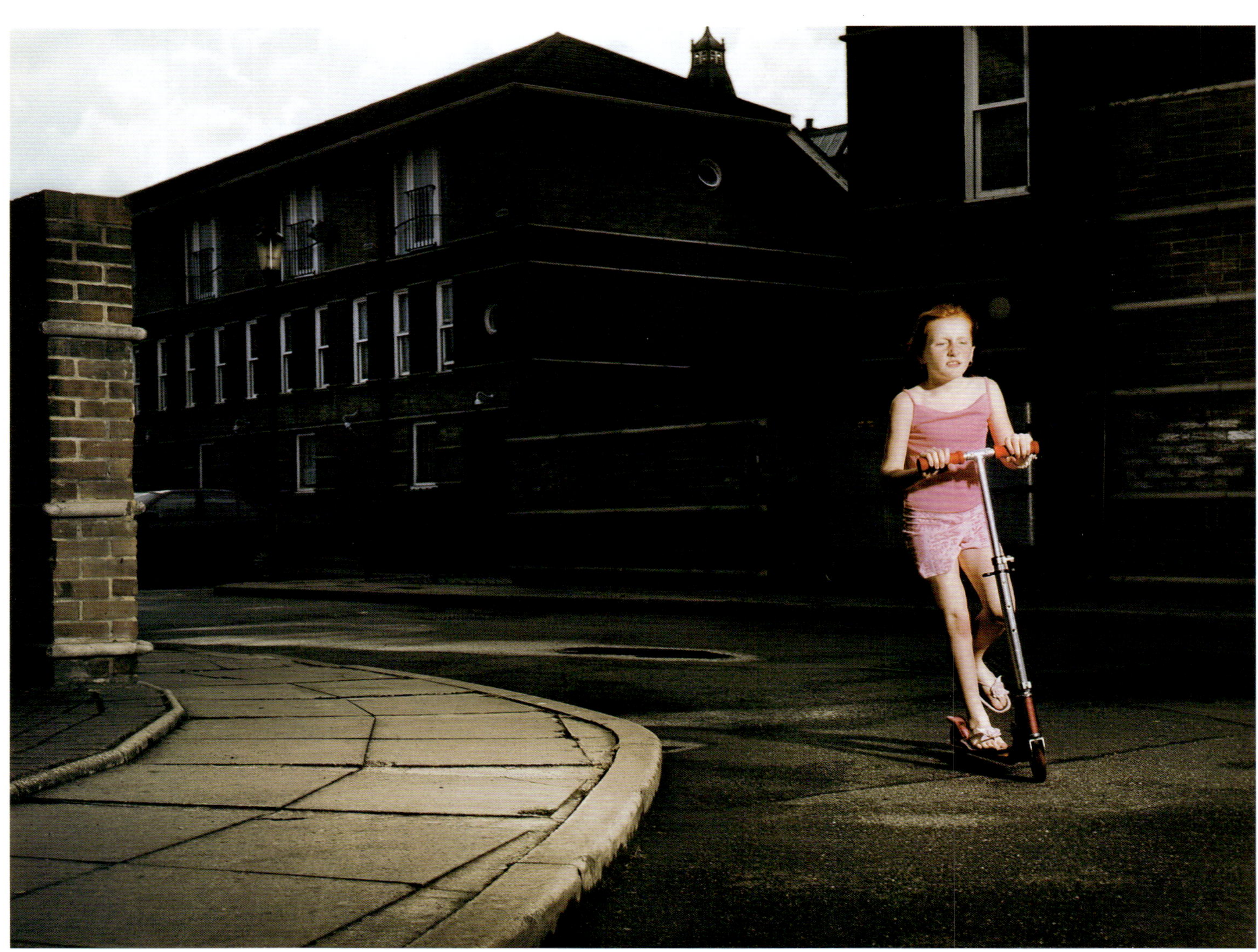

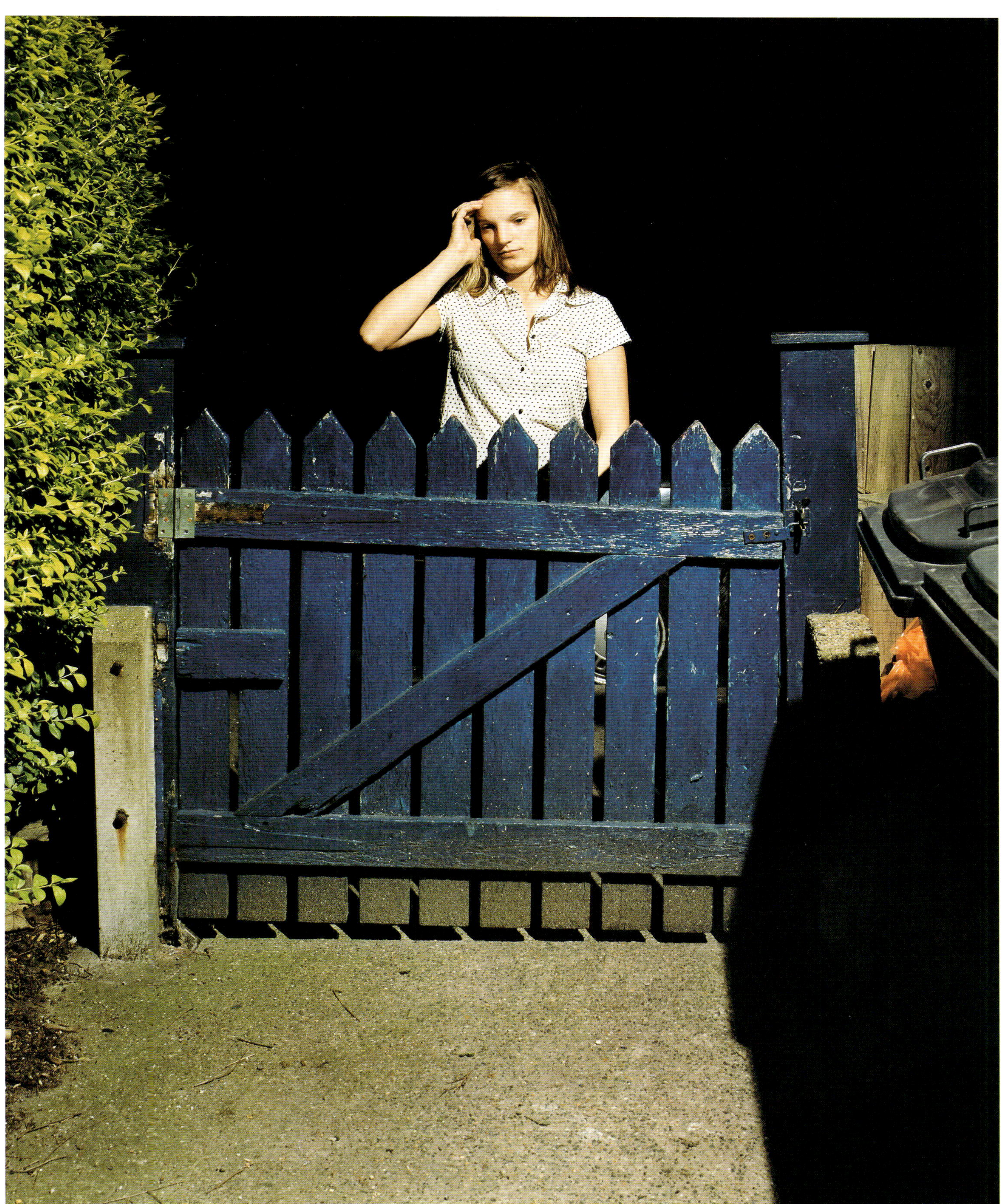

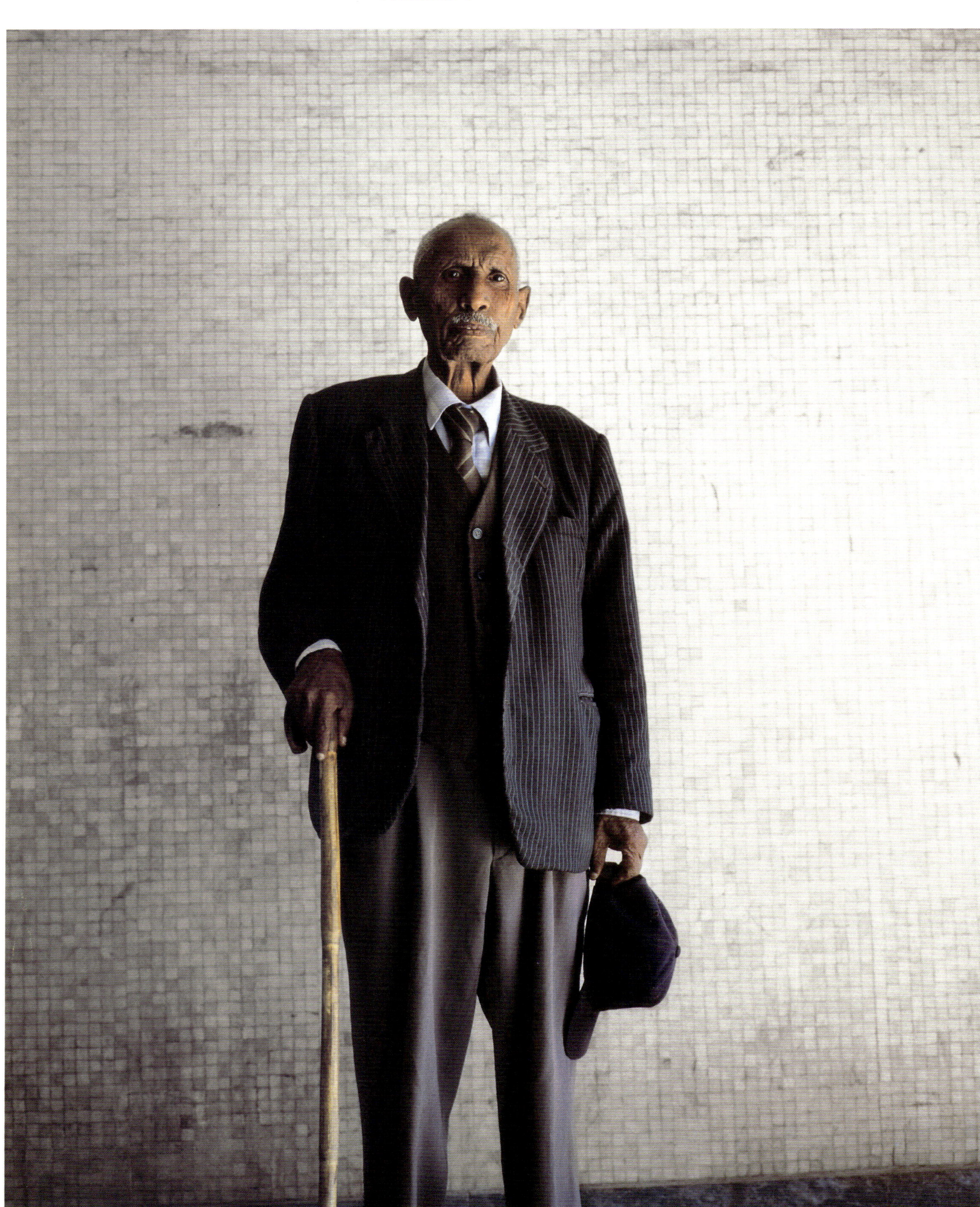

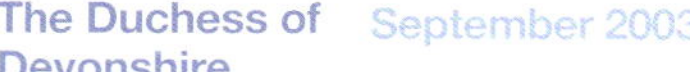

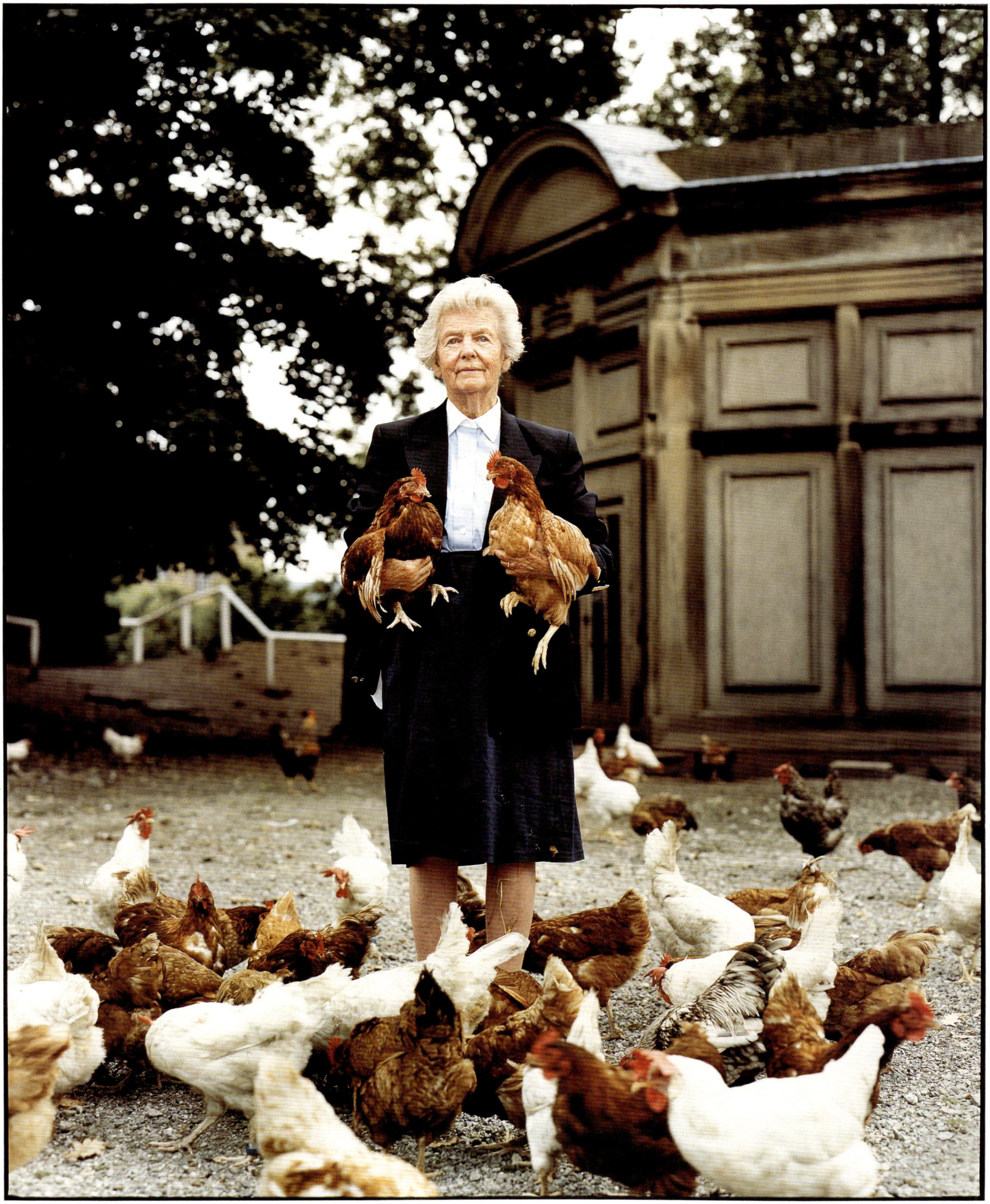

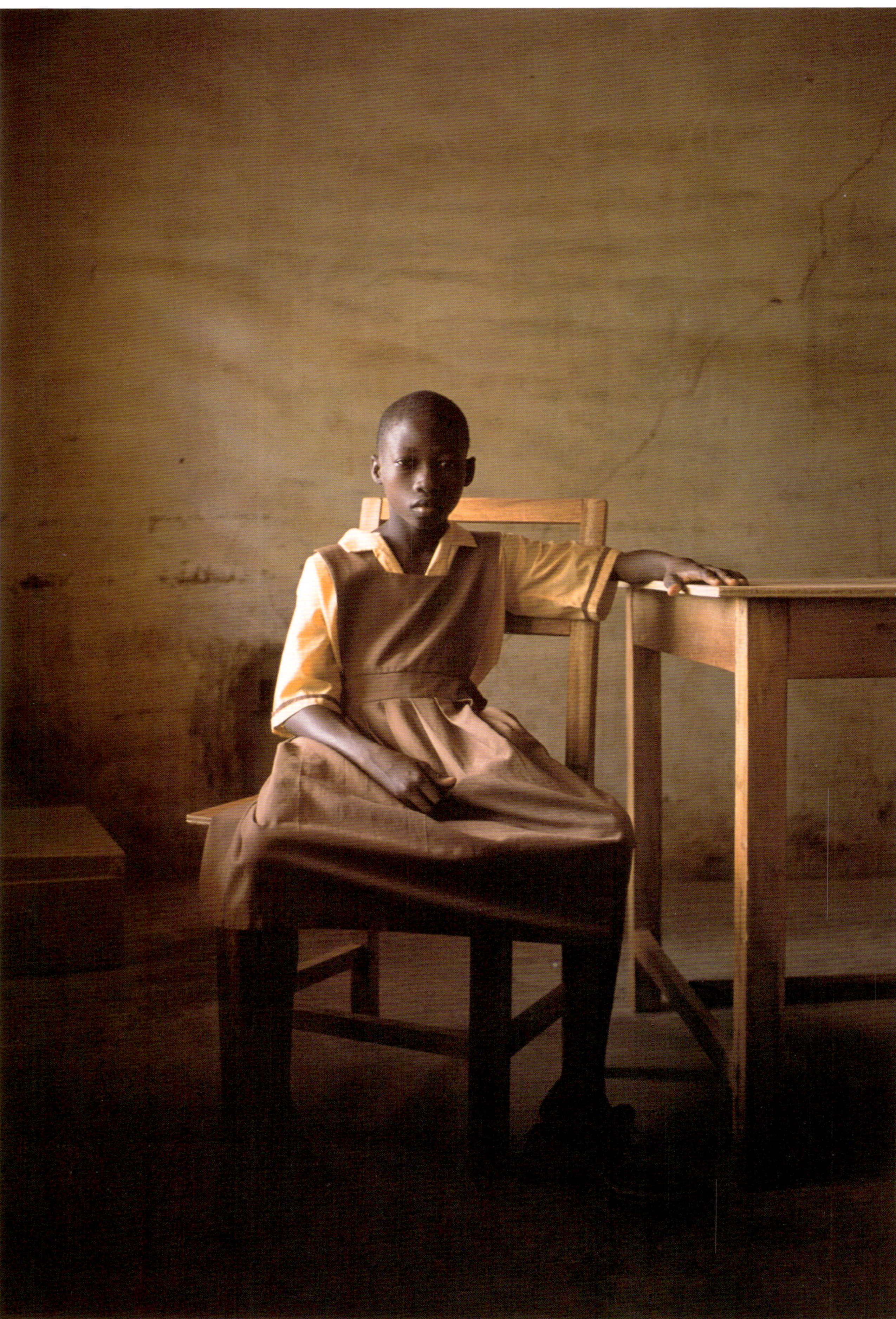

Opposite: Mark Manger
Charity Apibila; Aids Orphan – Bolgatanga, Ghana
November 2003

Steve Forrest
Murtza
July 2003

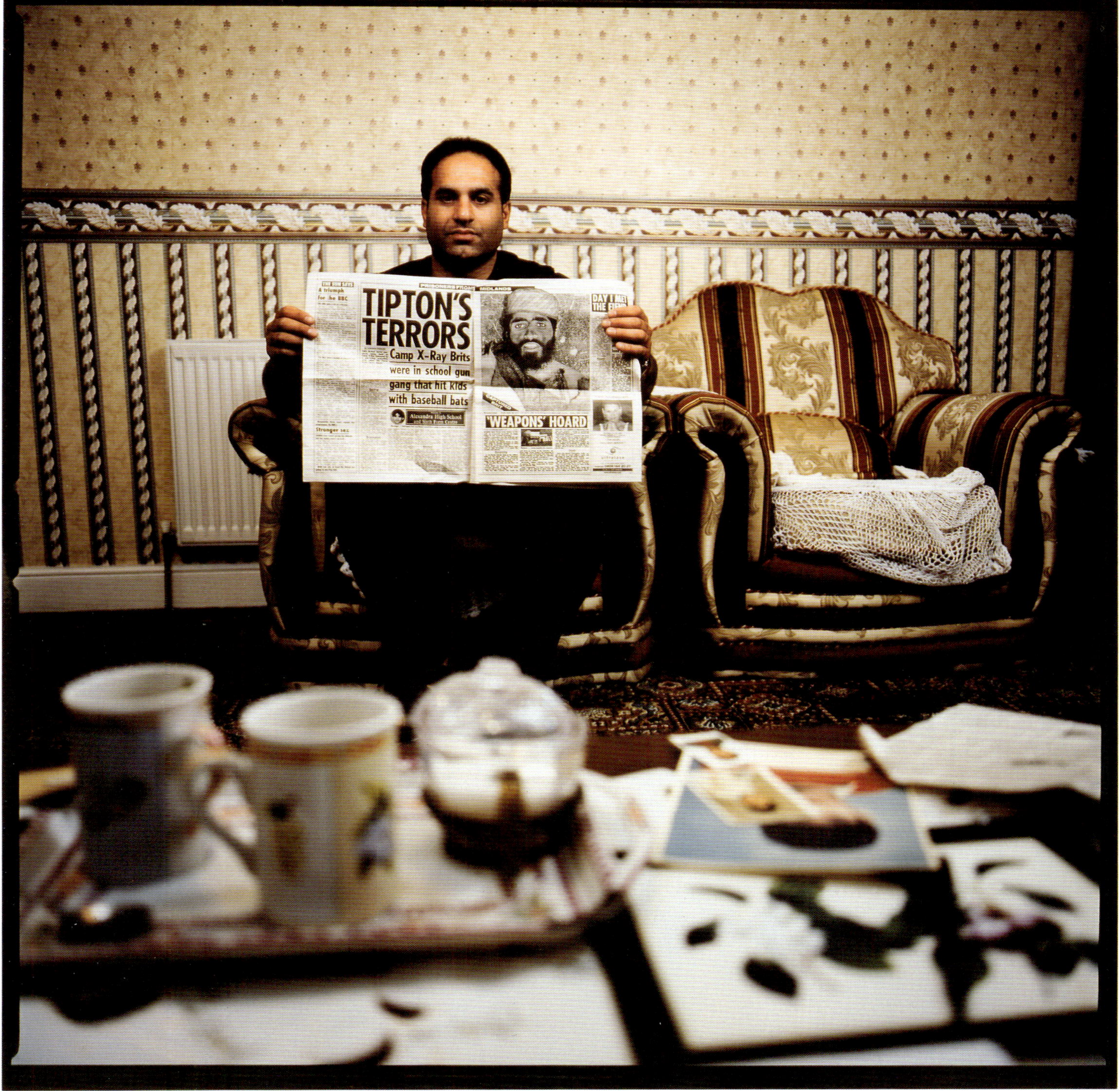

Jonathan Torgovnik

Twins #2 *from the series* Twins
August 2003

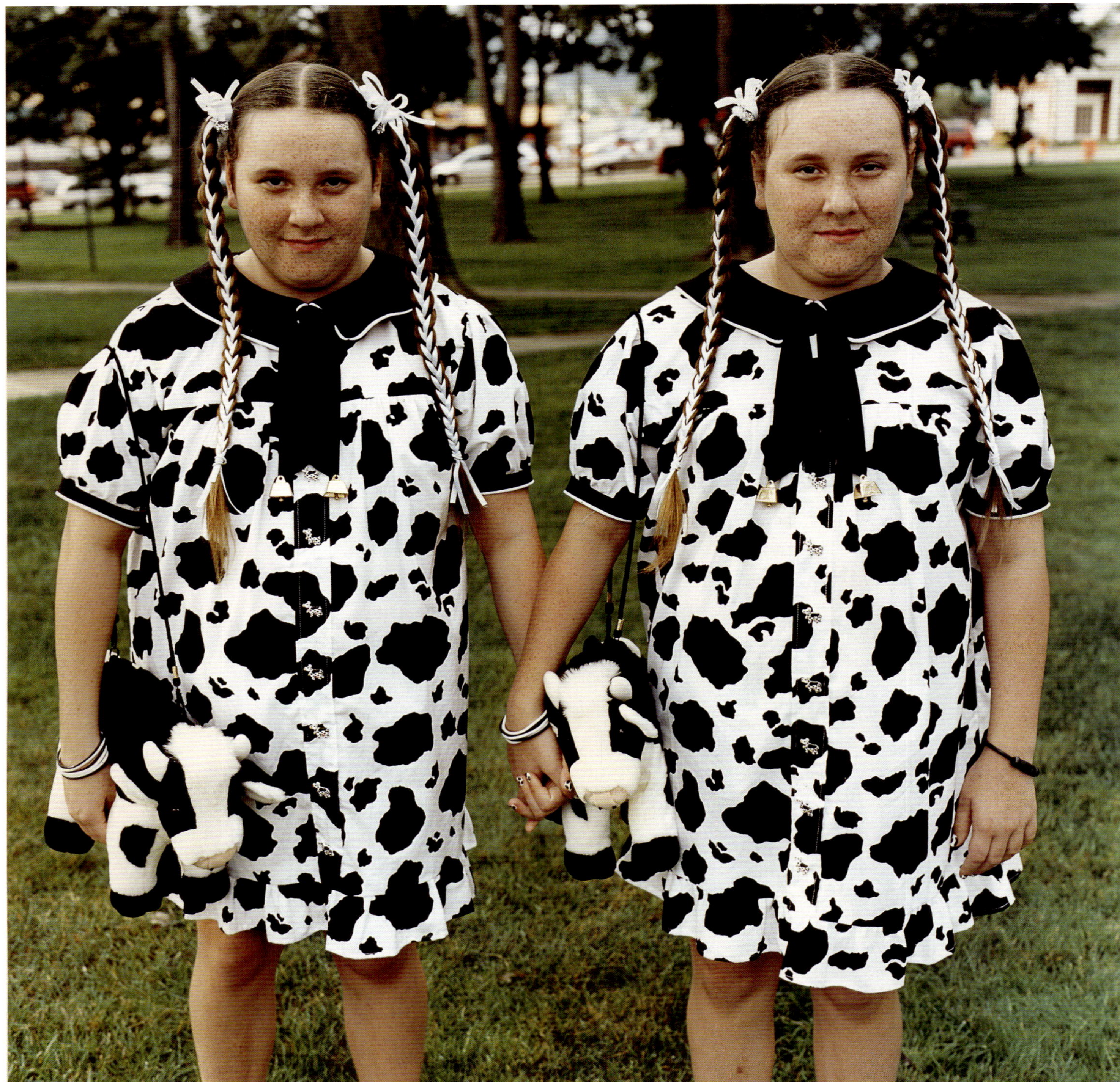

Jonathan Torgovnik

US Marines
Officer Course
March 2003

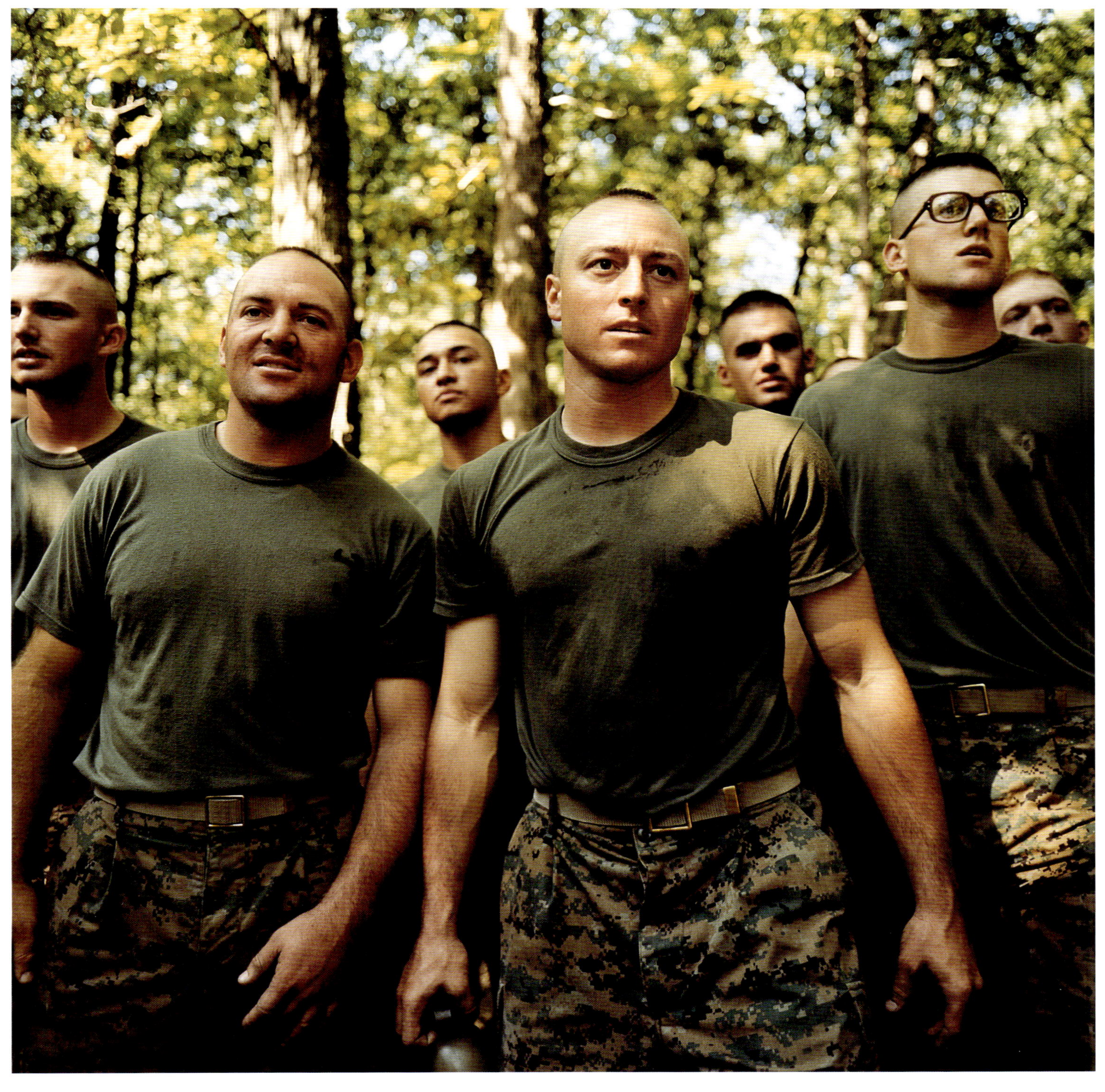

Peter Mallet

Mexican Street Photographer
January 2004

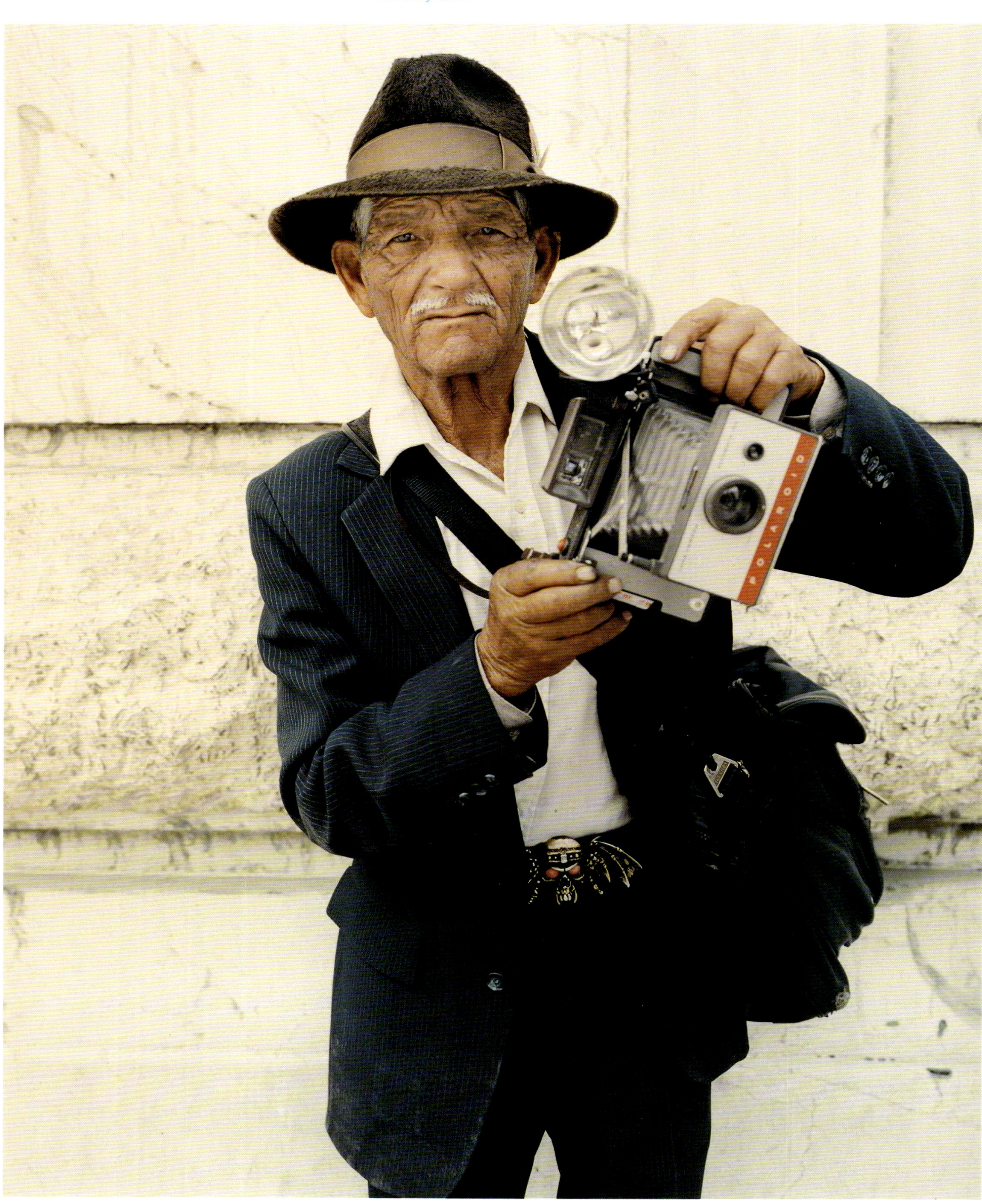

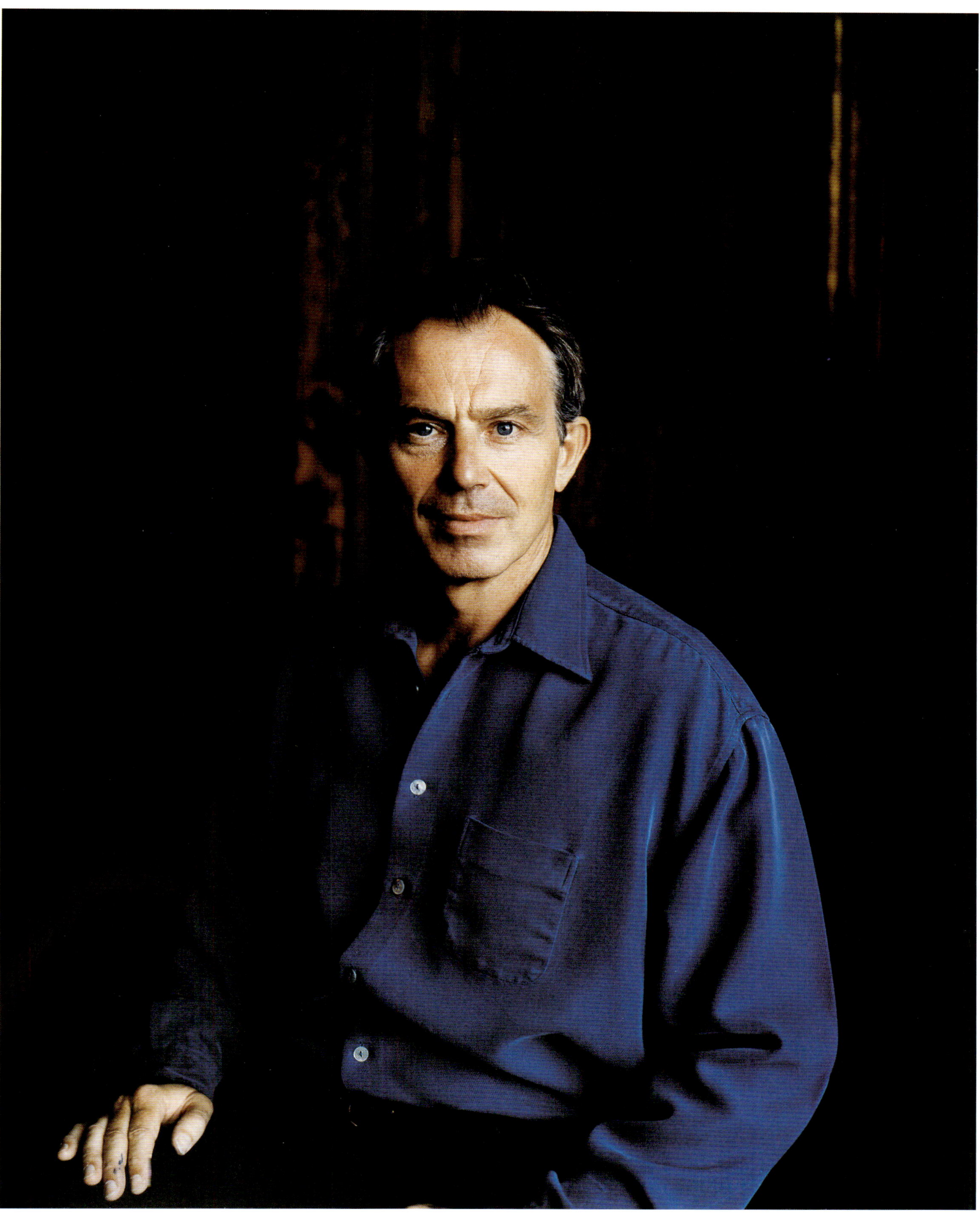

Lauren Shear

M.H. Wednesday 11.15am *from the series* Self-harm May 2004

Opposite: Nicola Kurtz

ZEBA – Attempted Homicide Survivor *from the series* Flames of Desperation October 2003

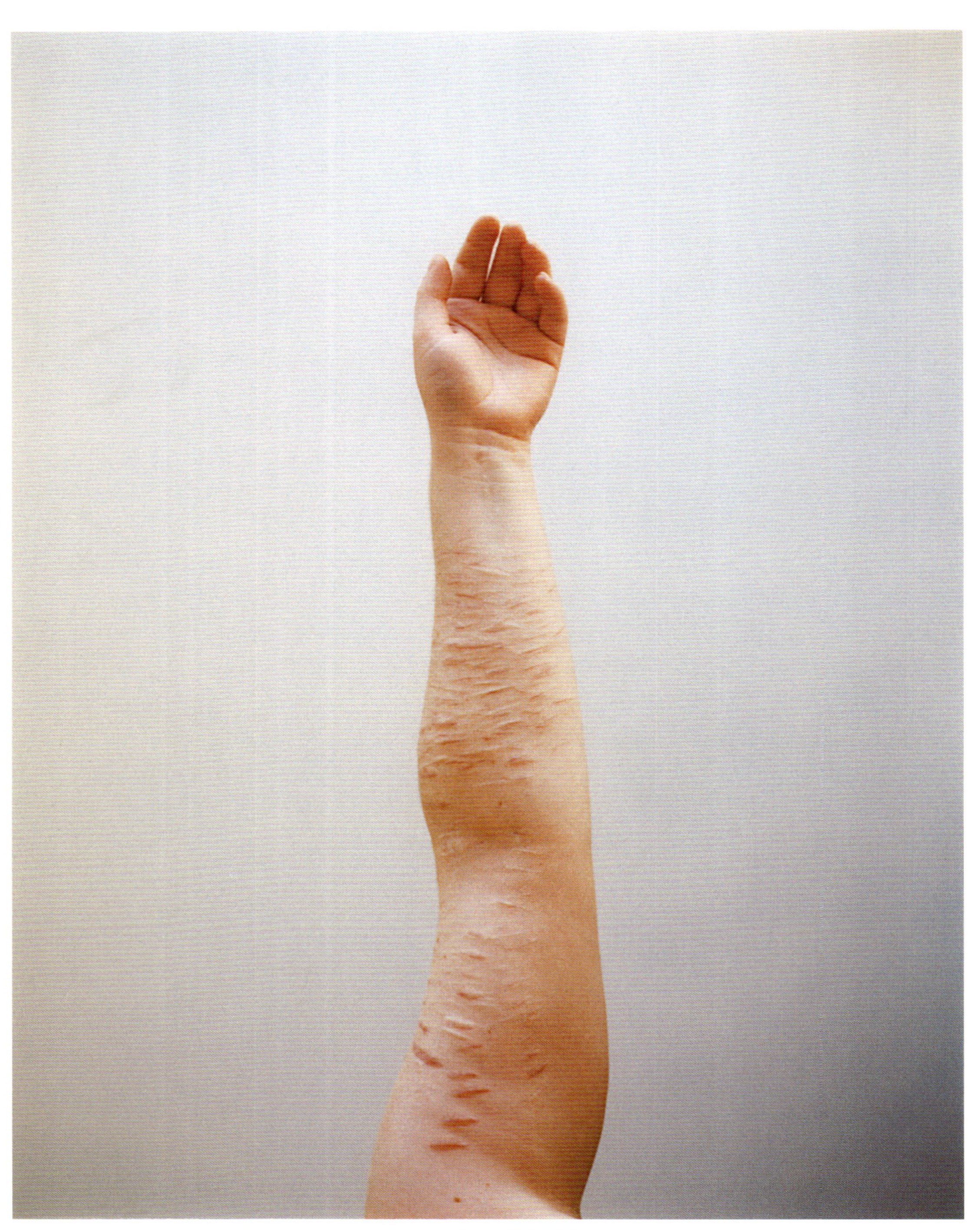

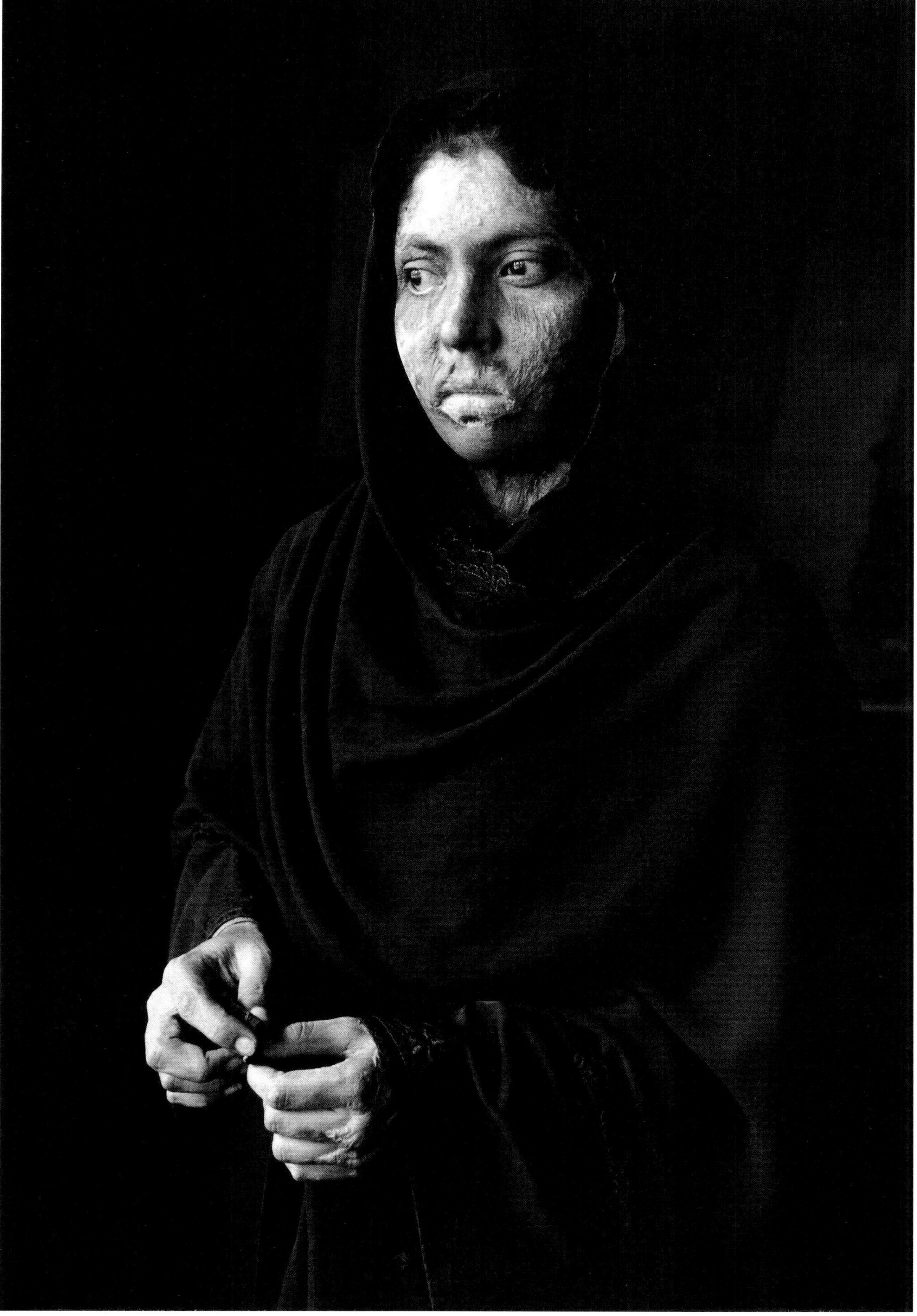

Michael Clement

Prostitute 2, Catonia *from the series* Prostitutes, Catonia
July 2004

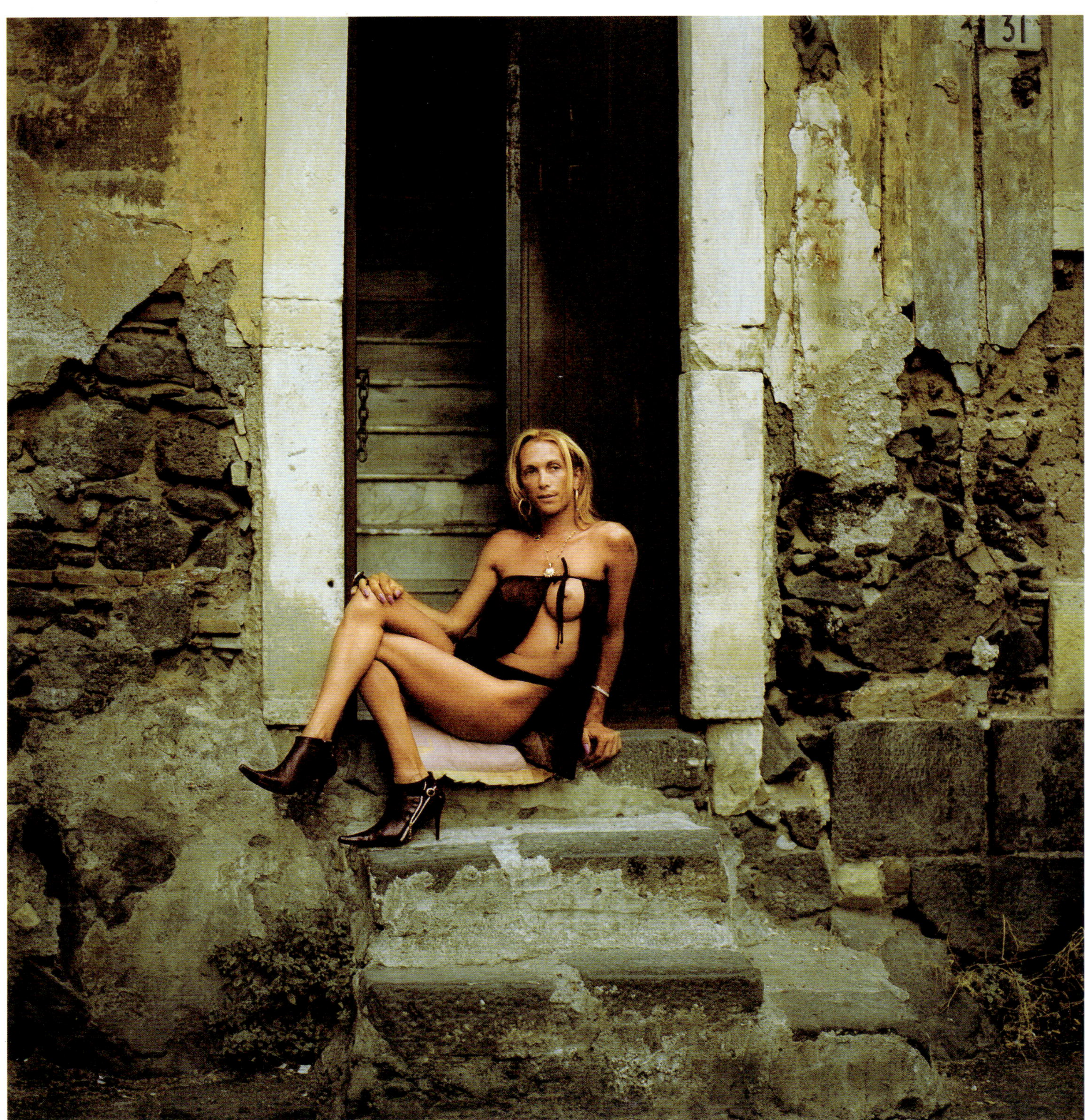